A BOOK ABOUT PRAYING

A BOOK ABOUT PRAYING

by
William J. O'Malley, S.J.

PAULIST PRESS
New York/Ramsey/Toronto

ACKNOWLEDGMENTS

The poem "no time ago" © 1946 by E.E. Cummings and the poem "i thank you God for most this amazing" © 1947 by E.E. Cummings and © 1975 by Nancy T. Andrews are reprinted from *Complete Poems 1913-1962* by E.E. Cummings by permission of Harcourt Brace Jovanovich, Inc.

The poem "The Red Wheelbarrow" by William Carlos Williams is reprinted from *Collected Earlier Poems* © 1938 by New Directions Publishing Corporation, and is reprinted by permission of New Directions Publishing Corporation.

NIHIL OBSTAT
Rev. Joseph M. Jankowiak
Censor Deputatus

IMPRIMATUR
Most Rev. Joseph L. Hogan, D.D.
Bishop of Rochester

June 22, 1976

Library of Congress
Catalog Card Number: 76-20954

ISBN: 0-8091-1979-X

Published by Paulist Press
Editorial Office: 1865 Broadway, New York, N.Y. 10023
Business Office: 545 Island Road, Ramsey, N.J. 07446

Printed and bound in the
United States of America

CONTENTS

For
William Peter Blatty
in gratitude
that we were brought together
by a mutual Friend

INTRODUCTION

Christian Doctrine vs. Christian Experience

A number of years ago, I wrote a musical called "Tender is the Knight." With mixed success, it was intended to be a satire on formal education, war, and other stupidities beloved of mankind. At the knight school, all the young men drilled and drilled and drilled every day to slaughter dragons—although none of them had ever seen a dragon. But there were always rumors. Meanwhile, up in the hills, the young dragons were snorting away trying to breathe fire and belch smoke in order to incinerate all those pink little knights—if they ever met one. Each side had heard such tales of the other! Of course, when a runaway young knight and a renegade young dragon meet one evening in the forest, they terrify one another half to death. But then, when they begin to talk as persons, when the things they've *heard about* each other give way to what they actually *experience* of each other, they become friends.

When I was young, a great deal of religious education was just that: arming our reluctant young minds with ammunition to refute the perfidious and

1

heretical arguments of those Protestants and Jews and Masons and Jehovah's Witnesses. There were whole armies of them, plotting to lure us from our side to their side. And all this despite the fact that many of our friends and neighbors and even relatives were members of these reputedly subversive groups, and there seemed to have been fewer religious arguments among the differing churches then than there are within the Church itself right now. Still, at least to my mind, that seemed at the time to be the whole reason for religious education.

Gradually, the churches saw how dumb the situation was and very wisely made peace. However, a great many American Catholics had defined themselves almost solely as being "not Protestant"; once that is taken away, what are we? And it is that loss of identity (which had been based on something so negative) that makes older Catholics nervous today. "With all this disrespect for the Pope, with all these free-thinking theologians, without Latin, we're just like the Protestants!"

A more practical and related problem, then, is: what do we teach our kids? The answers to that question have gone, I think, in two laudable but incomplete directions. One group uses banners, balloons and lots of love words; they show films about human problems, and have endless discussions of human values. All well and good, but so do pagans. The other approach—or the other "half" of the same religion teacher—exposes Christian doctrine: explanations of the Creed, the sacraments, the constitution and history of the Church, and (gasp!) year-long moral debates. All good and academic, but much of it would gladden the heart of the most fastidious Pharisee.

We have gone for the heart; we have gone for the head. But somewhere along the line we lost the thing that bonds the heart and the head together: the spirit, the soul, the self. We forgot that that whole list of doctrines in the Creed begins with: "*I* believe."

We've got impeccable human values; we've got marvelously organized Church rules. The one who got lost in the shuffle was God.

It seems to me we got so lost in explaining the signposts that point to God—the sacraments, the rules, the structures, even the Scriptures and the Church and the Mass—that we forgot to look in the direction they were all pointing. To a great extent, the God signs became God substitutes. We forgot to remember the Person who is the reason for all this fuss and, worse, we forgot to remember the reason he wanted all the fuss in the first place.

I trust God knew what he was doing on Mount Sinai, but it's too bad he had Moses come down with those two tablets of laws. People are so dumb—or so practical—or so wedded to the tangible and numbing numbers—that they focused all their attention on the two stone lists and forgot the light blazing from Moses' face, fresh from meeting God.

Jesus told us his purpose: "I have come to cast fire on the earth!" But as I look around at the Christian churches, I see lots of explanations and lots of debates, but precious little fire. He said: "I have come that they may have life, and have it more abundantly!" But as I look at my fellow Christians, I don't seem to see much more aliveness or joy or freedom than I see in my friends who are Jews or pagans or even atheists. There are even nominal Christians who tell me that what they wrongly think being a Christian means—all those rules and doctrines—are a positive hindrance to aliveness and joy and freedom. If that's what they think being Christian means, I don't blame them.

This calcification of aliveness into rule-keeping is not restricted to the churches. Education so often sets out to be an exciting attempt to enliven minds and ends up very pleased with keeping good order. Businesses so often begin with a pride-ful attempt to offer a quality product that will last and end up perfectly happy with making money. As John Gardner says, "The first sign of a dying society is when they issue a new edition of the rules."

Why does this happen? Perhaps because rules are easier to handle than love. Perhaps because doctrine is easier to teach than prayer. Perhaps because we are so conditioned to demand clear and distinct Cartesian ideas in classrooms, even in religious classrooms, that we shy away from introducing Christians to the Person who makes all the signs inadequate to capture him.

This book, inadequate itself, is an attempt to set up that meeting. It is an attempt on my part finally to begin doing what I was baptized and ordained to do: make my brothers and sisters come alive.

The Discursive Mind vs. The Receptive Spirit

This is a very dangerous book. At least I hope it will be dangerous, in the same way the Gospels are surely dangerous. It asks the reader to entertain the possibility that his or her life can be lived more intensely, but the price may be a lot of comfortable and protective habits and attitudes. But further it asks, at least as an experiment, that the reader surrender for a quarter-hour a day dependence on the discursive intelligence that balances budgets, works through assignments, figures things out. Instead, it asks the reader to open up powers of the spirit within him he may never have suspected, and allow the Spirit of God to take over.

The discursive intelligence is the power in us that analyzes, appraises, objectively judges. Most of our education is spent trying to strengthen it; people who can analyze well not only get good jobs but are far better able to cope with the problems of life. I surely don't mean to denigrate it; on the contrary, half my time teaching class is spent shouting, "Many men would rather die than think; most of them do!"

The discursive intelligence also has a place in the teaching of theology and Christian doctrine. The unfortunate thing is that, in my experience, it has taken over and dominates almost all of what is called religious education. Knowing *about* God has replaced knowing *God*.

For the most part, we don't know persons analytically. And yet God—who, we are told even in the most analytic theology class, is a Person—is treated as little more than a character in a novel or a figure in history. If he is to be known in any way other than the strictly and coldly academic mode, he has to be approached as we would approach any other person we want to know: as a friend.

But we are great talkers and rather poor listeners. Even in prayer, we want to dominate, to tell God something he doesn't know, and then be sure that the conversation is productive. What I am suggesting in these pages is that we give God a chance, too. So, for a few minutes a day, I am asking the reader to check his discursive intelligence at the door —all the itching to see the end, to get it over, to come up with answers, to capture everything in words and formulas. I am asking the reader to take the risk of being vulnerable to God.

The Exercises

Hopefully, the exercises in the following pages will be self-explanatory; in the very doing of them, their purpose should become clear. All they intend to do is set up situations where the person praying can become more aware of the presence of God at this moment than he ordinarily is. After that, the two of you are on your own!

But there are several warnings about these exercises that would be worth making. You will probably discover them for yourself, but there is no harm in anticipating them.

First of all, the exercises are not intended as a kind of spiritual cookbook: do this operation, stop, look at the recipe again, do that operation, etc. The easiest way is probably to use them in a classroom or group situation, one person knowing the progress of the exercise and in a very quiet voice suggesting the next step. But any of the exercises can be done alone. Read the exercise over; make a few notes if that kind of thing helps you; understand the progression, and then put the book aside and do it.

Second, find a place where you won't be interrupted or distracted. Later on, you may be able to withdraw into the deepest places in yourself with lots of people all around; but to begin it's best to start as simply as possible. Even if you are able to sit on top of a flagpole or in a cave in Tibet, however, you will have distractions—itches, remote noises, even the breeze, but especially from your own regular mind-set and memories: "Oh, I've got to remember to call Fred . . . Gee, that was a good idea; I must write it down . . . Boy, if I could only get Helen to have the idea I just got!" There are only two persons who should occupy your focused consciousness while you pray—you and God, and far less of you than of him.

If you are distracted—and you will be—you can gradually learn to catch yourself at it and return to the focus of the prayer again. This is one reason why the "trigger" for each prayer session should be very simple—no more than a few verses of Scripture, the single word "Jesus," even your own breathing—so that there is a simple, defined center to which you can return.

Third, make up your mind when you begin that you're going to sit there for fifteen minutes. Put your watch in your pocket and forget the bloody thing. Especially in the beginning, you're going to have ants in your pants; St. Teresa used to get up from her knees and shake the hourglass at times to make the time go faster! But even if it takes a certain quiet discipline to remain quietly and at peace, keep at it. After awhile, if things go reasonably well, you'll have to set an alarm clock to *stop* you! For all our talk about wanting peace, we find ourselves running pell-mell away from it. But it will grow on you if you give it a chance.

Finally, avoid assessing your progress. I know that some people suggest keeping a "prayer journal" to log progress and regression, but I personally think it is deadly. Prayer ceases to be a sharing of aliveness and becomes an experiment in which I myself am both subject and monitor. Don't stand aloof from yourself and say, "Hm. Look at me sitting here," or "Oh, I see! This is what's happening to me!" Far less should you think, "Oh, God! What would so-and-so think if he walked in and saw me doing this?" And never, never say, "Oh, well. That was supposed to happen inside me and it didn't."

Strange as it may sound to the discursive mind, you are not at prayer to learn anything. You are there to meet a Person. You are there to share love. You are there to share aliveness with God.

WHAT'S IN IT FOR ME?
—HUMANIZING

Aren't we all human already? Of course. It's perfectly obvious. We don't walk around on our knuckles; we're capable of thinking and of reflecting back on our own experience; we can anticipate the results of our actions, plan, hope, fear the not-yet-existent future. We're the only animals who can do those things; we're a different breed of cat.

But like the realization that we are indeed affected by the force of gravity, the realization of being human is something that sits way back at the outer reaches of our awareness. It's not something one focuses his attention on too frequently—which is why, I suspect, so many people end up acting *in*humanly: losing their tempers, cheating, shredding reputations, beating children, accepting war and slaughter as an unavoidable way of settling differences. Were we to reflect more often on our own humanity and the humanity of everyone we meet, there might be fewer prisons, fewer wars, fewer needless sufferers.

What's equally as bad, the rare occasions we

fall back on the term "human" occur quite often
only when we need justification for our own stupidity, as when we bungle and say, "Oh, well. It's only
human!" Which is like saying that being human
means acting stupid. Of course, there's a certain
amount of truth to that. We're not perfect; only
human beings need erasers. Only human beings can
be called on the carpet for doing stupid things. If a
puppy wets the rug or a sheep gets caught in barbed
wire, we may irrationally beat them, but they had no
idea what they were doing. If a normal adult human
being gets into a predicament where he wets the rug
or gets caught in barbed wire, however, he feels em-
barrassed. Even he admits with chagrin that it was
stupid. He should have known better; he should have
anticipated the consequences. Okay, so he's made a
dumb mistake, but it would seem to compound the
stupidity even further to shrug and say, "Oh, well.
It's only human!" Ordinarily when we say that, what
we're actually saying is that what we've done is not
human but childish or animal.

If being human means acting stupid, then what
are we when we're acting wisely?

To be fully human—as opposed to being childish or animal—is to know who you are and where
you are going.

Knowing who you are is a matter of sizing up
the world around you—the background, the context
by which you can see what the world truly is and
what life expects, with as little distortion of the truth
as possible and without defensive self-deceptions. It

also means making an honest assessment of one's own self—the talents and limitations, the susceptibilities to fooling oneself, the legitimate expectations and so forth—all the facets of one's body and mind and spirit.

Once a person has a calm and clear-eyed grasp of what the world and he himself seem to be—even if it is only temporary and inadequate—then he can begin choosing from the endless alternative ways of directing that one life he has. Knowing who he is, he can choose where he is going.

It is my contention that extremely few men and women do that. Far too many of the people I know sort of "fall into" a haphazard and hazy approximation of who they are and what life is for and where they are being led by life. It could hardly be called a "grasp," since that word implies some degree of sureness and control. It is rather more like a "touch" or a "suspicion" about . . . well, everything. As a result, such people let life "happen to" them. Like animals, they allow themselves to be led here and there, turned away from one path because it's too steep, huddling in fear of the elements and the boss's rages and their peers' expectations of them. They are far more like sheep than like human beings.

Laying aside for the moment any consideration of God at all, it is my further contention that, even as human beings, such people will never achieve anything remotely like a "grasp" of who they are and where they are going—in a word, of their own humanity—until they make the effort to find some time for peace each day, time to ponder, time to meditate.

Exercise

Find a quiet spot someplace and sit quietly, pondering that two-edged question: who am I, really, and where am I going with my life? Or if that seems too broad, then ask yourself the simpler question: am I really more or less in control of my values, my time, my goals, or is the control really "out of my hands"?

Simplification

We live in the most complex time in the history of humanity. Hurry, bustle, keep it moving, have it on my desk by yesterday! In every free moment, our senses are assaulted by billboards and ads and commercials shouting at us to buy this, buy that—or else! It's like being locked up in an asylum for insane carnival pitchmen—and yet we've gotten so used to adapting to it that we rarely realize how numb we have become. When we get home, the evening news presses our faces into the unending human sufferings and frustrations all over the globe, which men and women of earlier times were mercifully ignorant of—wars here, revolutions there, droughts and famine, the slaughter of orphans, kidnappings and rapes, tornadoes and floods. And the implicit question it calls up inside us is, "All right. The human family is no longer just the small group squatting together in your cave or your log cabin or your little village.

There are two billion of us out here, suffering. Are you just going to sit there and watch, or are you going to do something about it?" Leave me alone!

And all of this comes to us through a smothering, nerve-wrenching blanket of noise—noise from the radio, from the TV, from the record player; noise from the sirens of police cars and ambulances, from airplanes and trains and trucks; noise from people shouting to be noticed. Is there no calm eye in this hurricane of shrillness where one can find peace? Leave me alone!

And always someone is watching each of us, testing each of us: report cards, College Board scores, efficiency reports, traffic cops, tryouts and auditions and races. Who is the best? Who has the most dates? Who has the biggest chest? Who's playing quarterback and who is the Homecoming Queen? Who gets the raise? Is it any wonder so many people, young and old, feel persecuted and even paranoid? Get off my back! Leave me alone!

And while one is still relatively young, before he or she has decided to give in and stop wondering and live the zombie life, there is still the pesky question: why? Not merely why do I have to study math or why do I have to learn at all, but why do I have to knuckle under to "the way things are," why do I have to suffer, why doesn't anybody have the answers? And here is where the confusion becomes greatest, because there are so many voices which shout that they have *the* answer, *the* solution. "It's the lousy capitalist system," screams one. "It's the rebelliousness of youth and the permissiveness of the materialist society," yells another. "Drop out! . . . Get involved! . . . Smoke grass! . . . Go to Mass! . . . Demand your rights! . . . Do what you're told!" Leave me alone!

Is that all life is: working like an idiot fifty weeks of the year for the sake of a crummy two-week vacation? Is the secret just in developing numbnesses to the intimidating newscasts, the noise, the demands and competitions, the answers that are not answers at all? Where's the focus knob that will shift this kaleidoscopic complexity into something I can see as a whole, something unified, something with a clear and simple purpose? It's like being spun around until you're dizzy, and then opening your eyes to a maze of carnival mirrors.

The answer is simple, at least to say. In fact it was there, viscerally, all the time: leave me alone.

I am surely not recommending that each of us become a hermit—not as a complete way of life. In the first place, it's the rare man or woman who can take such a withdrawal; most of us need others. And in the second place, we not only need others but others need us. What I'm suggesting is that each of us also *needs*, at the very depth of his humanity, to become a hermit for at least ten or fifteen minutes a day. Unless there is an island of peace in the excited seas of our day, we will drown in the confusion and complexity and frustrations. Even though we may live on as benumbed zombies, we will die as human beings.

What does it cost to achieve a measure of peace, focus, simplification in the midst of a busy day? Nothing, or at least very little. All it costs is—for ten or fifteen minutes a day—letting go. First of all, one has to realize and accept the unarguable fact that he does indeed need a few minutes a day to achieve peace and perspective. Then one must actually stretch open an empty space in the unbroken succession of busy-nesses of the day in order to be alone. (And be reminded once again that I am not yet talking about praying or even about realizing the presence of God; I am merely speaking of the human need to re-collect one's self.)

Moving from recognition of the need to that initial decision to take the time, though, is far more difficult than I have made it sound. Even though it seems presumable that everyone, young and old, craves simplification and a measure of peace each day, actually taking the steps to achieve it is a "whole 'nother ballgame." There's just too much else to do, too many "important things." I'd like to, but I just can't seem to find the time.

But is that really true? It's the rare individual who doesn't have at least a little "fat" in his or her day: a couple of hours with the TV or record player or guitar, a half-hour with this one and then that one and then the other one on the phone, the Saturday basketball game or golf game, the coffee klatsch or the bridge game. There's no doubt that we all need time just to relax and "do nothing" with other people. But why don't we ever carve out fifteen minutes from our relaxation time to *really* relax, to do absolutely nothing but re-collect our selves? "Well, because I just never think about it—and, to tell you the truth, I'm rather afraid of missing something." Right. But if you don't take the time to meet your true self, you really *are* missing something.

If one of the children in the family falls down and cuts himself and starts screaming, somebody can always find the time to take care of him, even though it was an unexpected interruption. Why? "Well, because it's more important than anything I was doing at the time." Right. But when you take no time to assess your own inner hurts, they remain like a low-grade fever inside you.

Again, very few people nowadays—especially young people—have to be badgered into taking time to brush their teeth or take a shower. Why? "Well, because it's important, and it's worth taking the time to spruce yourself up. Getting your outer self together will very subtly add to your day and to your relationships with people." Right. But it's as important that your inner self also be "put together."

Whenever a mother mentions in confession that she has lost her temper with her children (and many young people would be startled at how invariably mothers accuse themselves of that), I always say, "For your penance, I'd like you to take a half-hour every afternoon just before the kids come home, sit in an easy chair with your feet up, with a cup of tea or a can of beer, and just relax." Believe it or not, some of them start to weep! Why? Because it makes such good sense, that's why! It's so obvious: rather than rushing around getting "things" ready before the kids come home from school, the mother should relax and get her *self* ready.

I've never had a mother disagree with the rightness of that "penance," but I can't help but wonder how many of them had the wisdom—and the courage—actually to *do* it. "Between the resolution and the act, falls the Shadow."

What I suggest—not only for mothers, but for stockbrokers and students and steelworkers—is fifteen minutes a day, not to "psych yourself up" but to psych yourself down. This means, only for those few moments, detaching oneself from everything that fluctuates and changes, and tranquilly resting in motionless repose. It merely means sitting in a chair or on the floor, or lying calmly but awake and aware, and letting it all drain out: all the confusion, all the deadlines, all the questions. Retreat from the bustle and obligation, and merely *be* there in the space— open, emptied, at peace, receptive. It is not the time to try to "solve" anything. It is merely the time to re-collect one's peace and perspective. The "solving" can wait fifteen minutes—and the man or woman facing a question after a few minutes of peaceful withdrawal will be far more likely to find a truer solution.

It is not the poets and contemplatives who go crazy, as Chesterton said. It's the "solvers." The man or woman who tries to bring an intensity of intelligence or emotion to a problem usually ends up with teeth gritted so tightly that his or her fillings fuse together. Life is an infinite sea, but the man or woman who is trying to "solve" everything is trying to cross an infinite sea, thus witlessly trying to make it finite. But the poet and the contemplative float easily on the infinite sea and enjoy the view. They have found peace.

Exercise

Rather than merely reading *about* the effects of a few moments of peace, why not try it?

Find a place where you're pretty sure you won't be disturbed by radios or traffic or people. Put your watch in your pocket or purse.

Sit down with your hands resting quietly in your lap. Let yourself relax. Close your eyes; take a deep, deep breath. Hold it for a second or two, then let it go— and let all the tension go out with it. Roll your head around slowly from shoulder to chest to shoulder to back until the tension goes out of your muscles. Then let your head sag to your chest or hang back.

Let your shoulders sag, and let the tiredness and tension sink down through your wrists, into your legs, and through your bottom into the chair. Let it all sink down and empty out; imagine the tiredness like waves of heat or energy draining down through your legs and through your feet into the floor or the ground. Gravity is pulling all the tension and worries and deadlines out of you for a few minutes.

Just sit there with your mind quiet, let-ting your imagination travel again through your empty head and down through your empty shoulders and back and chest, your empty arms, your empty pelvis, your empty legs. If you have to say something to keep the focus of your concentration, just say over and over quietly in the deepest part of yourself, something like: "Peace. Peace. For these few moments, there's nothing to worry about, nothing to bother about. Peace. Peace."

If it's easier in the beginning, lean forward with your elbows on your knees and your forehead and cheeks resting on your hands. Relax. If you start to feel tension or distraction, take another easy deep breath and exhaust it with the breath. Relax.

Read the directions again. It's really quite simple. Just draining out all the busyness from top to bottom, and then resting in that peace, assuring yourself that the world can do without you for this little while. Let it last as long as it will.

Now, try it.

* * *

If you're like many people, once you've read this page, you'll say, "Okay, I got that," and want to move on to see more —or get the rest over with. But you haven't "got it" till you've tried it. For yourself. Try it.

Awareness

When you're walking along a busy downtown street, how much do you see of what's going on? Relatively nothing, actually. There are almost an infinite number of stimuli bombarding our senses— hundreds of people, hundreds of stores, hundreds of vehicles, hundreds of signs—clamoring for attention, and in order to preserve our sanity, we automatically put up protective "shields," a kind of screen that will let only those stimuli pass through which we can tolerate. It is a kind of built-in, self-defensive "simplification."

The trouble is that our senses are assaulted so often during the day, not just on the streets but in the office, the classroom, the home, that we keep the shields up even when there is relative calm—like someone with arms raised to ward off a blow, even when he is alone. As a result, we are in danger of losing perception of anything gentle or commonplace. Unless food is burning hot or music is earsplitting or colors are blistering, they have very little chance of getting through the shields. Consequently, we are often aware only of the surfaces of life—and only the most blatantly obvious surfaces at that.

Unless one is in love with another person, who notices the color of his eyes or the part in her hair or the textures of the skin? Such picky attention to trivial details is apparently unimportant, and one usually has at least a vague, hazy "picture" of his acquaintances. But isn't that almost like looking at all but one or two people in one's whole life with the reception "out of focus"? And how many millions of potentially fascinating people does that leave "tuned out" completely? If we were to approach even a few more people in our small circle with the same intent awareness we approach someone we love ardently, how much our lives would be enriched!

A heightened awareness of the rich facets of life is another answer to "what's in it for me" if I take a few minutes each day to find peace and perspective. If there is a place in my day where I retreat, withdraw into a few moments of unbothered restfulness, the rat race slows down, the pressures that hold up the shields ease off. Even a few moments of "psychological distance" allows things to fall back into their proper sizes.

One day a very good friend of mine was grading *Macbeth* tests at his desk when his little daughter came up and said, "Daddy, Daddy! Come quick! The roof! The birds!" But he was up against a deadline; he'd promised his students he'd have the papers back the following day. With hardly a look at her he said, as so many parents do, "Not now, honey. Daddy's busy." He went on with his work, hardly remembering that she had even bothered him, when suddenly he was aware of her standing next to his desk, a big fat tear running down her cheek. In that moment, he really saw her. Wisely, he got up and let her lead him by the hand to the apartment window, and for ten minutes or so they looked out at the birds on the adjoining roof. They weren't "accomplishing" anything, but something was happening.

In that moment of clear vision, things had fallen into their true perspective for him again. *Macbeth* had lasted for 350 years; but his daughter would be filled with wonder for only a few. Robert Frost's poem, "Stopping by Woods," which every school child has heard fifty times—and rarely listened to—says the same thing: "The woods are lovely, dark and deep./ But I have promises to keep." There is no time to see things; only time to do things.

William Carlos Williams has a poem that attempts to pull us up short with the same need for awareness and for putting things back into perspective:

> so much depends
> upon
>
> a red wheel
> barrow
>
> glazed with rain
> water
>
> beside the white
> chickens

Not only does taking time to reflect put the outside world into perspective, it also allows us—for a rare moment in the day—to come into contact with the deepest part of our own selves. We become so caught up in the surfaces of ourselves, the things that ads want us to worry about—the lines on the skin, the acne, the odors, the clothes—that we neglect the deepest places of who-we-are.

The human person is an iceberg with only a fraction of its massive reality protruding above the surface. It's hard for us to imagine the enormous power that lurks unsuspected beneath the iron doors that separate our conscious selves from our subconscious selves. And it is perhaps in those unprobed depths that the Spirit of God dwells in us.

But even limiting our attention still to the purely human sphere, we see there is a power of spirit deep within each self that we are lured away from tapping because of the innumerable calls on our time and on our purely surface awareness. If only we could focus on one surface—like my friend with his little girl—and let its inner truth enter us, perhaps we could turn the same awareness into the deeper parts of ourselves and contact a source of aliveness we have been carrying around, unnoticed, all these years.

Exercises

1. Begin with the relaxing exercise given earlier in the chapter.
2. While you are sitting there relaxed and "away from the world" for awhile, hold some kind of natural object on your lap —an orange, a rose, a stone, a plant— and absorb it with your consciousness. Study its veins and pockmarks, its texture and its weight. Give it the full focus of your relaxed attention. Then let your imagination roam: Where did it come from? Who has handled it before? What keeps it going?
   The purpose of this part of the exercise is not a botanical or geological study but merely to give a point of focus to your relaxed contemplation and, even if only for a few moments, to heighten your awareness of the innumerable facets and fascination of a single natural object in this innumerably faceted world of ours.
3. Then set the object aside and shift your heightened attentiveness to some part of yourself—your hand, your heartbeat, your breathing. Let your attention rest inquiringly on the same physical tex-

tures and rhythms as with the nonhuman object. Then quietly, peacefully dwell on the same questions: Where did this come from? How does it keep me going?

This part of the exercise, too, is not a scientific inquiry but merely an attempt to reflect peacefully on the incredible complexity of this body that carries us about, takes in information, shapes our communications with other human beings.

Feeding the Spirit

The human person is not some kind of tripartite complex of three separable blocks: body, mind and spirit. It is a living intermesh of all three of those realities, and no scientist or philosopher can tell you where the body's functions end and the mind takes over, where the mind and body fall away and the spirit is free to soar beyond the limits of time and space.

And yet each of the three aspects of human activity can be studied by itself, setting aside momentarily the other two, as long as we realize the dependence of each on the others. Surely the body of man has all the properties of any other animal body: it takes up space, it moves us from here to there, it needs food and oxygen and rest. The human mind on the other hand, even though it is dependent on the body and will be affected by the body's condition, has a measure of control over the body and its functions. What's more, as the body is meant to cope with space, the mind is meant to cope with time:

remembering, recognizing, making judgments, computing, planning, and so forth. Its processes are localizable in the human brain.

But there are other activities of the human person that, though dependent on the body and mind, do not seem to be strictly limited to them or by them. There is some aspect of the human person that seems able to work even *counter* to the mind and its logic. We see this when someone falls in love. Why care so crazily about this person? Why this person and not another? And that love cannot be given full expression by either the body or the mind. It is in this area of human activity that we "hope against hope," that we trust one another, that we rejoice, that we cope with mystery, that we feel the wonder and ecstasy that lets us swing free of body and mind.

This latter group of human activities is the one that, it seems to me, the present world is slowly, witlessly starving to death.

The human body is fed with the bodies of other animals, with the vegetation of the earth, with air and sunshine and so forth. The human mind is fed with information, with the evidence passed on to it by the human bodily sensors, with the experience other men and women compress into words and share with us. And just as the body's sensors feed the mind, the products of the body-mind feed the spirit. But the activities of the spirit—love, hope, faith, mystery—are beyond the scope of either the body or the mind. Love, hope, faith and mystery cannot be boxed in by logic or by weighing or measuring or timing. When the spirit is active, it is to some extent able to leap free of time and space, free of body and mind.

When the body is hungry, it lets us know, and it gurgles and grunts tyranically until we feed it. The human mind's hungers are signaled by curiosity—the itch to know, to uncover, to see behind the closed door. But the demands of the mind are more easily avoided than the demands of the body; inertia very often puts the book back on the shelf, moves the fingers out of the dictionary, reaches for the knobs of the TV and contents itself with passively ingesting mental baby food.

The body gurgles, the mind itches, and the hunger of the spirit expresses itself in restlessness and discontent. But it is very vague and formless. It is not as easy to pin down as the rumblings of the belly or the curiosity of the mind. The body can shift position when it is uncomfortable; the mind can sit down with a book or a pencil and paper or a more knowledgeable teacher and figure out problems. But the restlessness of the spirit is usually caused by questions for which there seem to be no cut-and-dried answers: why doesn't she love me, why do I fail even when I try my damndest, whom can I trust, where am I going, what's it all about? The human spirit is fed on peace and joy—and there seems to be precious little of either in our world today.

In the hurly-burly rush of work and noise and distractions, where can the human spirit find peace? In the indifference, the plastic, the numbing routine of the days, where can the human spirit find joy? The love of a few close friends gives some measure of both, but it is so transitory, so infrequent, that the human spirit is in danger of withering and leaving the human person little more than a computer carried around by a hundred pounds or so of sensitive flesh.

Many people feed this hunger of the spirit with art. For those who understand and are willing to take the time, the moments spent absorbing a painting in a museum or watching bodies move in a dance or being filled with the music of a concert orchestra or sharing life in the pages of a novel are moments that uplift the spirit and feed its hunger for peace and joy. The arts are not in any sense "useful"; they cannot be weighed or counted; they cannot be stored away as so much useful information. Although the paintings themselves or the theatre tickets or the books can be sold and bought, the experiences themselves cannot. And yet their effect is obvious in the placidity and ease of those men and women who are able to be peacefully absorbed and at rest in art. Their spirits are alive.

Exercise

1. Begin with the relaxing exercise. For a few moments, let the world slip away.
2. Take a book like Edward Steichen's *The Family of Man* or LIFE's year-end picture collection which show truly human beings caught at special moments in their lives. Pore slowly over each picture in its turn, without any hurry to "get through" the book, pausing and absorb-

ing yourself in the picture and its inhabitants for as long as the picture still feeds your spirit. Try to know them—their pain, their joy, their humanness.

The same kind of restful absorption can take place in the most peace-less places —a busy street corner, the lobby of a hotel, an airport waiting room. Merely sit quietly, as if you were invisible, and watch the faces, the ways personality is expressed in movements and reactions, the hundreds of human lives that are as filled with their private joys and sorrows as yours is.

Wisdom

Everyone knows that there is a qualitative difference between wisdom and knowledge. They are related to each other: wisdom has something to do with what you know, but it seems to go—well, farther. When you've got a problem for which there's a definite, clear-cut answer, you go to someone who has knowledge. When you've got a mystery on your hands, like "What's it all about?" or "Where is everything going?" or a question for which there seems no apparent answer, you go to someone who has wisdom.

Anyone can accumulate facts if he or she has patience and a retentive memory. This ability of the mind is an ability the mind shares with a mechanical computer: taking in and storing data, manipulating it logically, and coming up with answers. But this is precisely where the mind and spirit differ. Knowledge and logic are qualities of the mind; wisdom is a quality of the spirit.

Rather than define what "wisdom" means, it might be better if each reader paused a minute and tried to think of someone in his or her own experience who was "wise." Think about it for a moment. Usually it is someone a bit older; wisdom has something to do with experience, with having-lived-a-bit. But all older people are not people we would call wise; accumulating experiences isn't the only element of wisdom. Neither, necessarily, is the number of books one has read. There is a *quality* about wise persons we know that has nothing to do with the *quantity* of years or experiences or degrees. There is a sense that this person has assimilated the meaning of his experience and reading, grasped its inner core, made it part of himself. The reason one feels confident in listening to that person's advice is that the wise man or woman has a kind of assurance, a calm and peaceful *possession* of the truth, and he or she can discern more clearly and judge more soundly what is true and false, what is right or wrong, what is truly important and unimportant, what will lead to joy and what will lead to self-destruction. The man of knowledge wants definite answers, and he is angry at uncertainty; the man of wisdom is searching, too, but he seems far less afraid or upset by uncertainty.

Wisdom, then, has something to do with experience-reflected-upon. But if one is so busy doing and experiencing that he or she has no time for quiet reflection, then life becomes not a connected whole seen with realistic perspective but merely one-damn-thing-after-another.

Such people—most people—endure the intermittent sufferings of their lives with the dumb confusion of animals, weeping, gnashing teeth, crying tormentedly, "Why me!" The wise man or woman has achieved a certain perspective not only on the sufferings of others but, more importantly, on their own. Because they have taken the time and effort—and pain—to face the sufferings of life rather than run away from them, they understand more clearly that sufferings are unavoidable. They understand, too, that there are some unpleasant facts of life that neither they, for all their efforts, nor science, for all its cures, nor prayers nor groaning nor rebellion will ever uproot or change. The child born mongoloid cannot be restored to normalcy; he or she can only be loved. The alcoholic cannot be convinced by all the arguments in the world; he can be loved, reminded, refused the victory of ruining others' lives. The wantwit spendthrift cannot be taught budgeting and caution; he can only be loved, tolerated, allowed to hurt himself till he gets some measure of wisdom or dies.

The wise person knows that all the progress in the world will never make evil go away. There will always be unkindness and selfishness and death. Sorry, but that's the way things are.

In a word, the wise person knows that there is no god but God. Science is not God. Progress is not God. Money is not God. And most important, the wise person knows that *he* is not God.

That sounds rather silly. We all know we have our shortcomings; we all know we are not God. But do we? Don't our actions—the grunting and groaning, the search for "the answer" when absolutely nothing can be done—really belie our claims that we are not God? Don't our actions really say, "I *can* find the answer, even if there isn't one! I *won't* accept the fact that I am limited!"

In accepting the inevitable, the unchangeable, the wise person accepts the true perspective of things, his or her position in the ascending order of beings in the universe. He or she is better than a rock or a carrot or a pig; he or she is less than God.

It is surprising how much less such people seem to suffer. At times the wise person seems almost callous—refusing to sob or screech or swear revenge on the universe. Instead, he rides out the storm with a kind of placid detachment which seems, to the insensitive, to be insensitivity. It is not that at all. It is like—on a much lower and more mundane level— the person who goes to the dentist, sits back in the chair and says to himself, "I know from experience that this is going to hurt. Okay. But I also know from experience that I can get through it."

Somehow, such a person actually experiences less physical pain than one who tenses up, tightens, as if there were some way he or she could avoid the unavoidable pain. The same thing occurs in childbirth when the expectant mother has been schooled to expect and accept a certain amount of pain in labor. But for the mother all tensed up and ready to defend herself, fear multiplies the actual pain a hundredfold. The analogy can be extended, I think, to any pain at all—feeling unwanted, failing at a job, losing a loved one in death. The wise man or woman struggles might and main to avoid pain, but when it is demonstrably unavoidable, he or she says, "This will hurt, but I can endure." As a result, they suffer less than those who whine or rage at the inevitable, and shake their fists at a silent sky, shouting, "How can a good God do this to me?" As if they expected an answer.

Wisdom does not come from suffering. If it did, animals in experimental laboratories would be wiser than all of us. Wisdom comes from suffering reflected upon and accepted and assimilated. The wise man or woman does not have answers or "solutions" to suffering, but they know what the truths of human life are. Somehow they have used reflectiveness not only to heal their minds but actually to take their suffering and turn it into their strength.

Such wise people are, in the fullest sense of Thomas Harris's term, Okay; they are Adults. The inner self can serve as a calm mediator in the inner combat between the whimpering, raging rebellious Child on the one hand and the finger-wagging, fault-finding Parent on the other. The wise man or woman is free from the domination of either. And yet, at the same time the wise one can admire and use the values of both the Child's simplicity and awe and candor and the Parent's order and discipline and demand for progress.

But without time to achieve perspective, the self will be dominated by the slings and arrows of outrageous fortune that assault him from the outside and will be dominated by the civil war between the Parent and Child inside. If one is to achieve self-possession, if one is to achieve wisdom, he must first conquer the demand to rush around constantly, to escape the facts of human life. He must take time to withdraw from the transitory in order to discover the permanent.

Exercise

1. Before doing the usual relaxing exercise, focus your attention on some problem you have—a feeling of inadequacy, a constant weakness, some kind of lack or loss—or on a really stupid and hurtful mistake you have made. Then, when the feelings about it become intense, do the relaxing exercise.
2. Then, take a picture book like Steichen's *Family of Man* or LIFE's year-end best pictures and, in that quiet, meditative mood, turn the pages slowly until you come to a picture that holds your attention. Pore over it, absorb yourself into it. Then, with this event still filling your inner self, quietly compare your original problem with this one. Very calmly put the two events—your problem and this catastrophe—into comparison and perspective.

   You may not yet have actually accumulated much experience, but the experience of others can provide a vicarious experience that your imagination and your own sense of compassion can make a very real part of your own experience.

Freedom

Most people who don't think too deeply or too often think that true freedom means the ability to do

absolutely anything one wants, without restriction—
even without the restriction of our actions' natural
consequences. And they yearn for that kind of freedom, ache inwardly and endlessly for it. To put it
concretely, I think it often means that such people
want to be so rich that they can get away with anything. Their hearts rebel against the petty but tyran-
nous demands of the boss, the teacher, the spouse,
the parent. They grind their teeth at the unfairness of
things—that the wicked prosper while the honest go
hungry; that the rich, the beautiful, the charming,
the talented are fawned over and rewarded while the
flawed—most of us—are condescended to or passed
by unnoticed, on the way to someone more interest-
ing.

But few of us will ever be so rich that people
will not be free to refuse us their love. They may
pander to our desires in order to collect their pay,
but we cannot buy their inner acceptance of us with
money. If such were the case, there could be only
one person free and all the rest would be his slaves,
not only externally but internally too. If someone
were to achieve that power, it would be a "gift" as
deadly as King Midas's. When love is not freely
given, it is no longer love.

Actually, the content of the idea of "freedom"
that such people vaguely envision and so frustratedly
long for seems to be not really the desire to be
"free" but the desire to be "sovereign"—without any
higher power than oneself, with nothing above one in
any form that might hinder him in any way. This is
manifestly impossible—even for kings, even for bil-

lionaires, even for czars, sultans and emperors.

Even Ghengis Khan was *subject* to the law of gravity. He had to submit, as humbly as a child, before windstorms and earthquakes and floods. Whether he wanted to or not, he had to eat, defecate, sleep, have toothaches, grow weary. There was a limit to what he could drink without passing out or getting sick. He was locked into *this* time and *this* place and *this* self. If one were the emperor of all the world, with all the money, all the power, he would still be as powerless as a peasant in the face of death.

So often people say, "If only I had been born at that time," or "If only my parents had been such-and-such." Those two words—"If only"—are the two most wasted words known to mankind, since whatever follows after them is almost always utterly impossible. And yet how subtly but deeply we are enslaved to those impossible words.

All right. So everyone will grant, in his saner moments, that there are certain things over which no human being is sovereign. What we mean then is really that we wish we could be free of criticism, free of the demands and expectations of others. Admittedly, most people I know are too subject to what others think of them but, unless you are willing to go off and be a hermit, you are never going to be free of criticism or demands or expectations. To live in any society—whether in Nazi Germany or in a Colorado commune, whether in the ordinary family or in Hell's Angels—means automatically to set up a web of relationships, of interlocking expectations and responsibilities. Even two people alone on a desert island have their freedom limited by the fact that another depends on them. Either one or both may not like it, but that's the way things are. Either one is free to kill off the other, overdemanding one, but the inescapable consequence (from which he is not free) is that he must then live alone.

To love is automatically to surrender a part of one's freedom to the beloved, who can call on one's time and effort and concern even when it is inconvenient.

Freedom, then, is not the ability to be untouched by the pressures that a physical life on earth imposes on all of us, from peasant to president. Nor does it mean being untouched by the limitations that living together imposes on all of us, from Hippie to Hitler. I think true freedom really comes from knowing and accepting the truth—the way things really are—no matter how unpleasant, and acting accordingly with complete peace of mind.

For such a desirably positive idea, freedom is actually a very negative thing. If you check a dictionary or a thesaurus, you find that every single synonym for this positive goal has to be given in negative terms: *not* subject, with*out* restrictions, *not* determined, *un*controlled. And such words most often describe a state of freedom from *external* limitation —like gravity and report cards and prison bars. But the real freedom, the freedom that can survive any external limitation whatsoever—even death—is *internal* freedom.

A man or woman can be forced by external pressure to get up at a certain hour, do such and such work, forego the fulfillment of dreams, put on a happy face. But inside, he or she is still free to think and believe whatever he or she wishes.

A man or woman is also free to stand up against those external pressures whenever he or she chooses freely to do so—provided he or she is willing to accept the inevitable consequences. One can stand up and tell the boss or teacher to go to hell, but he then has to pay the piper. One can refuse to tell government secrets even under torture, but the alternative is that the torture will go on. One can sell all he has and give to the poor, but he will have to get along, then, without a Dispose-all and a stereo.

Granted that there are restrictions on all of us, it is astonishing that people so rarely use the freedom that they actually do have. It is pitiful how much undeserved abuse we will take when we have the freedom to say "Stop!" It is silly how many hours we will neutralize our powers in front of a television set when we are free to do so many other things.

But is that quite true? In a sense, the TV addict is free to go for a walk, paint a picture, go to a ballgame, mow the lawn, pray—or a hundred thousand other things. But is he *really* free? Whenever the recess bells rings in the school where I teach, the seniors—even the ones who don't smoke—automatically head for the lounge, with as little choice as iron filings in the presence of a magnet. Many times in the day, each of us is free *from* any external demand to do some particular task. The question is whether we are free *to* do anything other than the habitual things, the things "we always do at that time." Freedom-from is not automatically freedom-to.

In order to be free from our own *self*-imposed limitations, we must first be aware that there are actually alternatives, and have some idea what those alternatives are. I have to laugh when I hear young people angrily demanding, "I want to be free to be who *I* am!" But when you reply, "Of course you are. But who *are* you?" they usually slump glumly and say, "I dunno." Freedom is very sharply curtailed most of the time by one's own ignorance.

I suspect that one of the reasons we become so addicted to our habits is that they make things so much easier. We don't have to think at all of what else we could more profitably—and even more happily—be doing as long as there is the TV knob handy; the only choice is which program we want to bore ourselves with.

Calculated ignorance of alternatives minimizes one's freedom not only in trivial situations, like how to spend a couple of "free" hours, but also in crucial situations, like which college to choose, which spouse to choose, which line of work to choose, which religion to choose. If a boy, for instance, knows of only one or two colleges, one or two girls, one or two professions, one only vaguely inspected religion, his freedom is scaled down to the absolute minimum. The less you know, the less confused you are—but also the less free you are. You are not free to choose an alternative, no matter how beautiful or fulfilling, if you haven't taken the trouble to discover that it exists.

Furthermore, when one justifies his so-called "choices" with such statements as "Oh, well, everybody cheats," or "That's what 'they' all say," he is not acting freely at all. His actions are enslaved to "everybody" and "they." I have to laugh when some unmarried people say that the Pill gives them freedom, since these same people, given the right comeon, are free to go to bed with so-and-so but not really in any sense free to stay *out* of bed with so-and-so. When I see the seniors I teach going off to college, I realize very candidly that they will be free to stop going to Mass, sleep around, cheat, get stoned. But I have to wonder how many will be truly free—from the external pressures of their peers and from the inner pressures of their own susceptibility—to enjoy Mass, be chaste, be honest, be sober. Freedom is not freedom when, realistically, this is the only thing I am capable of "choosing."

I suspect that the best word I can think of as a synonym for "free" is the word "unbiased." To make a truly free choice, one must be unbiased by external pressures, unbiased by his own ignorance of the other alternatives and the consequences of each, but most importantly unbiased by internal pressures: irrational prejudices, clinging to previous habits, self-protectiveness, fear of losing what one surely has now in the hope of some not-so-sure benefit in the future.

All these internal obstacles to truly free choice

can be boiled down, I think, to fear. "But what will happen to me if . . . ?" The boy or girl trying to make a firm decision to give up drugs or masturbation or cheating or casual sex may have no pressure from outside sources whatsoever; say, for the sake of argument, that no one else even knows about this habit or, if the only other participant knows, not only will not tell anyone but positively wants the practice to continue. It's possible—in fact very often is actually true—that the individual also knows full well where this situation is leading, what the inevitably painful results are going to be; ignorance of the alternatives and their consequences is no obstacle to free choice. What does inhibit a free choice is fear: how will I get along without it? I'm only *betting* that living without this thing will be better, right? I have no way of being utterly certain I will be happier and more humanly fulfilled without it.

It's like standing on the edge of an icy pond on a hot day. No one's going to push me in. I know a refreshing swim is what I want. But still I hesitate, clinging to the dock. I'm attached to the security of my present discomfort; I can't freely leap into the water for fear that what I will find will be worse than what I have.

St. Paul said it as well as anyone: "The evil that I do not want to do, I do; the good that I want to do, I do not do."

How, then, does one remove these irrational attachments that prevent him from making a free choice? The answer is logically simple: you detach yourself from them. Sounds easy, huh? We all know, though, that it's not.

In his little book of retreat meditations, *The Spiritual Exercises*, St. Ignatius Loyola makes fundamentally the same assertion as the Buddhist mystics about the only way to make a perfectly free choice: become "indifferent." By that he means, choose the alternative that is the truth—which means the same thing as the will of God, since God sees things as they most truly are—without any fears or irrational prejudices or biases. In every decision, choose the truth—no matter what the good or bad consequences to oneself.

This presumes, of course, that one realizes that the universe revolves around God and not around the individual self, that the relative merits of one choice over another depend on the way things really are and not on the way I personally feel about them at the moment.

This "detachment" and "indifference" do not imply that the person must become insensitive. Nor does it mean that one must become heedless of the way this decision will affect others—in fact, very often, putting one's own self-protectiveness completely aside will reveal for the first time how one choice will save the pain of others, even at a cost to oneself. "Detachment" means that one chooses without possessiveness, without self-serving ambition, without impulsiveness, without greed. It is concerned only with doing the truth, and counting the cost later —if at all.

Perhaps the easiest way to see this is by an analogy. The person who makes the freest decision, the detached decision, brings himself to the point where he can honestly look at this problem as if it were someone else's problem; he has studied all the elements of the choice and, without fear of what it is going to cost him-as-advisor, he cool-headedly offers the best answer.

St. Ignatius has at least two exercises that are intended at least to show the retreatant what detachment and true freedom really mean—even if the retreatant cannot personally bring himself to make such a free choice in the case of his own particular attachments. Perhaps it would help to clarify true freedom if I proposed them here as exercises. If you personally at this time feel that you are enslaved to something, they may help. If not, they will at least clarify the notion and serve as a logical bridge from this chapter to the next, from what's in prayer for me as a human being and what's in prayer for me as a child of our Father.

Exercises

(Do either of the two exercises after reading them both. Then read the section from St. Luke at the end, *after* you have done the pondering.)

A. *The Ten Thousand Dollars*

1. Perform the usual relaxing exercises, and at the same time try to focus your consciousness not merely on the inner center of yourself but on the Spirit who dwells within you at that most central place.

2. Imagine that, through some perfectly honorable means like a will or the State lottery, you have come into $10,000. The money has been delivered to your house in cash. You are all alone with it. (No external pressure.) Feel it with your hands: one hundred $100 bills. Weigh it. Feel the texture of it.

3. Then think of all you could do with this money. Explore them all, even writing them out on paper. (No ignorance of possible alternatives.) First decision: will you use the money all or in part for yourself? What will you buy for yourself? What will you use it to pay for? Second decision: will you use this money in part or totally for others? If so, for whom? And how far will that circle of generosity extend: just to your family, just to your close friends, even to strangers? How would the percentages fall?

   Remember: to be detached from prejudice, you must not be swayed by selfishness. On the other hand, you must not be uncritically swayed by the feeling that one should be guilty about spending money on himself. Money is not evil or good; only the use of it is one or the other.

4. Now, in your imagination, see yourself taking the entire bundle of bills in your hands again. Feel them. Now, in your imagination, see if you can picture yourself taking that stack of bills and placing them on the altar in front of the tabernacle. See if you can picture yourself backing away and saying to God, "Okay. What is the *best* choice? What is the way to use this money according to the way things really are, according to the way You see things?"

5. Rest there a moment—looking from some distance at the pile of bills resting in front of the tabernacle. What are your inner feelings—in your gut, in your hands? How truly free are you?

B. *The Deathbed*

As in the first exercise, you can use this meditation on an imaginary but fully real-ized $10,000. If, on the other hand, you actually have a decision to make or some activity to be reassessed for continuance or uprooting, use that. In the exercise itself, I will use the example of the money, and you can make your own substitutions if you choose.

1. As usual, relax and bring your consciousness to bear on the center of yourself, becoming aware that this place is where your aliveness verges on God's aliveness.

2. Imagine that today you have come honorably into $10,000; it's delivered to you alone; you feel it, weigh it, make it real for yourself. You are trying to make up your mind what use or uses to put the money to. As in the last-suggested exercise, stay there awhile, weighing the possibilities, the pros and cons. (Or if you are working through an actual personal decision, consider all the advantages and disadvantages of the alternatives you have, along with the consequences of each alternative to you and others. Even write them out if that is an easier way to keep them separate and clear.)

3. Now switch the scene in your imagination to the future. It is thirty or forty or fifty years from now. You have lived your life with the consequences of that very important choice you made years

before. Feel yourself lying on the bed, the texture of the blanket and sheets, the light and odors of the room. At that moment before death, what would be the choice you wish you had made?

Against the background of a whole lifetime, that choice scales down into a more proper and true perspective than when one faced the choice in the excitement and pressures of the moment. And against the background of death, that choice will be rendered unchangeable. In that very real-ized setting, which choice do you wish you had made all those years before?

*   *   *

When you have actually finished either of the exercises—and only then—ponder the following section from Luke's Gospel (14:12-14) which, we trust, is what the God-Man would have done with the $10,000. "Then [Jesus] said to his host, 'When you give a lunch or dinner, do not ask your friends, brothers, relations and rich neighbors, for fear they repay your courtesy by inviting you in return. No. When you have a party, invite the poor, the crippled, the lame, the blind; that they cannot pay you back means that you are fortunate, because repayment will be made to you when the virtuous rise again.' "

WHAT'S IN IT FOR ME?
—DIVINIZING

One can humanize himself; that is, he can enrich and deepen and intensify his possession of all that it is to be human, if only he is willing to take the time to reflect and possess his human heritage. But no one can divinize himself. The Roman emperors tried, with disastrous results. People in mental hospitals sadly convince themselves that they are God or Jesus or Buddha, but no one pauses to worship them. The very idea of a human being becoming godlike is about as unthinkable as a rock beginning to wander about or a turnip singing "The Star-Spangled Banner" or a monkey typing a rough draft of *War and Peace*. No individual being on the scale of beings— mineral, vegetable, animal, human—can hoist himself up by his own bootstraps into the next higher level of sensitivity and activity.

But word is out that a man named Jesus Christ did that for us. As the story goes, the Son of God— limitless, immortal, unhindered by time and space— surrendered all that to become human. He did it in order to let us know that, through him, we could become divinized: the sons and daughters of Almighty God. That is the Good News of the Christian Gospel: that we need not fear annihilation at death, that he and his Father are willing to share their Spirit, even now, with us if we are willing to receive him. In Christ we can become godlike. There is no bootstrap effort on our part to *cause* this divinization; all we need to do is recognize the gift and accept it.

Like all gifts, the gift of divinization can be refused and therefore, for me, "it doesn't work." But the heartbreaking part of such refusals is that the gift of a share in the aliveness of God is usually rejected without the potential receiver even looking it over. It's like the woman whose rich great-aunt died and left her nothing more than a boring old piece of furniture. Angry at being cheated when she expected so much more, she pitched the dumb thing out without appraising it, without realizing that it was a priceless antique worth thousands. Similarly, many of us were led to expect far more of religion than what we seem to have gotten: catechism answers, moral strictures, and an hour of boring, repetitive, stultifying ritual every Sunday morning. So, angry at being cheated, many of us pitch out the whole God "thing" without even appraising it, without realizing its priceless worth.

Part of the reason for this foolish self-impoverishment is that appraising anything takes a bit of effort and time—not much, but more than we are willing to take from the headlong rush. What's more, if one hasn't made the effort to become even fully human, he will not even be able to see that being Christianized and divinized actually is a value. He will be too contentedly locked into the plastic placebos of the TV and record player.

And so he fumbles through what he thinks is his tiny life, as oblivious of his own possible greatness as the young Helen Keller was of hers.

The Wider Context

We have seen already that as human beings we tend to pull back for security into far too tiny, far too self-centered lives. Without a realization of the immensity of the world and its sufferings, our own little sufferings tend to get inflated out of proportion, assuming an importance and intensity far beyond their causes. But when one sees them in the perspective of the slaughter in Vietnam and the starvation in the Sahara, our own little headaches and disappointments can't help but assume their true size. Our pains and problems are very real, of course, but far less dramatic and earth-shattering than they seemed when our focus was on our own little corner of the world rather than on the wider context of the whole human brotherhood.

Imagine, then, how much less significant they become when seen against the background of all human history, and even less against the background of our own immortality and the endless dimension of God. When the old monks went to their superior with some petty complaint or some bickering difference of opinion, the wise prior would often say, *"Quid ad aeternitatem?"* That is, "What significance has this event got when seen in the light of an endless and eternal lifetime?"

Such a realization is dangerous, however. It is undeniably true that being turned down for a date or missing out on a promotion—or even the death of a loved one—diminishes to near-insignificance when seen in the context of all the people who died in the world today, or all the people who have died since the world began, or the eternal life that death cannot end. Still, such a realization can convince one that nothing he does has any objective meaning at all in the long run, that he is—to all intents and purposes —utterly negligible when seen against that background. In a sense, that is absolutely true and unavoidable. But in another sense, it is not true at all.

The Good News of the Christian message does force us to see ourselves as infinitesimally small, like one single drop in the endless ocean of reality. And yet it also says something startlingly contrary to that: *despite* our seeming insignificance, the God of the Universe—for reasons only he can tell—finds each of us incredibly important to him. As the Scriptures say, he calls each of us by name; if he cares for the lilies of the field, how much more does he care for us; like a Good Shepherd he is willing to leave the ninety-nine and come searching for the one who is lost. Now there is News to be reckoned with! We are, on the one hand, lost in the anonymity of billions upon billions of beings. But on the other hand, we stand out in the eyes of the limitlessly loving Father.

In looking beyond our parochial little neighborhoods, we see that the immensity of the universe is all one. The atoms that make up fire and mountains, cabbages and tigers, asteroids and suns, are the same atoms of which I am composed. I take them into me in food and air; I expel them and they return to the one Whole. We all share the same "stuff" in our make-up and in our continuance.

And yet in the eyes of God I am an identifiable part of this immense Whole.

Exercise

(This is an adaptation of an Iranian *sufi* meditation.)

1. Do the relaxing exercise first, but bring it to a climax with a realization that in that still center-point of yourself, you verge into the presence of God.

2. Sit in this peaceful quietude before a lighted candle. Absorb yourself in the flame, calmly, focusing all your attention on the light. If you haven't a candle, close your eyes and imagine a circle of light with a point of light in the middle of it. Let your imagination "draw" a circle around that point of light, and then let the candle flame or the light point expand in your imagination to fill the circle around it. (This isn't easy, so don't try to rush it.) When the light has filled the circle, let it contract very slowly again into a point, then very slowly swell to fill the circle again. The light is like the invisible-but-truly-present atoms which bond the air and the flame and the candle together.

3. Slowly let this light spread out beyond the imaginary circle around it and fill

the room or the space you are in. Let it penetrate and fill your body and your mind. Let your whole self be absorbed into the light. (This, too, may take time. Don't try to rush. Don't go on until you somehow feel deep in yourself this union, this being-filled-with the light.)

4. Then let your imagination expand the light from this room and yourself first out over the whole building, the whole city, the whole country, the whole globe. Rest in that for awhile, knowing that you are a part of this greatness of light.

5. Let your imagination swell out further as the light spreads to the whole universe—this immensity of union, bonded piece-to-piece by the invisible atoms. See both the limitless expanse of the light but also the focus of it emanating from you in this room with this candle. Rest in that realization for as long as it contents you, as long as something is "happening" within you.

6. Finally, let the light break through the barriers of time and space into the immeasurable Light who is the Source of our light, of our shared existence. See in your imagination the widening circles of light from this candle, from yourself, this place, this world, this universe out into the endless depths of God. Rest easily on that infinite sea of Light, knowing you are fused with it and yet not absorbed, still a self, a droplet-point in that endless sea of existence. Don't speak unless you must. Just be-with.

Re-read the suggested directions and try it. Don't rush. Don't have any expectations. Easily. Peacefully. Calmly.

The Vitality Beneath Everything

I have a rather well-founded suspicion that the reason many young people experiment with drugs is that they *know* there is a greater aliveness lurking beneath the seemingly impenetrable surfaces of things. Surely there's more to life than the plastic-coated throwaways we spend our hard-earned pennies for. Surely there's more excitement and joy and even pain hiding behind the everyday masks of indifference on the people we elbow past on our way to . . . where? I feel rumblings in the depths of my own person which tell me that even the surface self I've been willing to look at and tolerate is sitting on a very volcano of aliveness within me, which I am afraid to see and rejoice in and set free. A time of contemplative quiet would put me into at least the beginning of a contact with that powerful aliveness beneath the surface of myself and other people and the whole universe. But taking that meditative time is repugnant to one who is always in a rush, and I find it easier to plunk down a few bucks for some grass or pills to give me a chemical shortcut. Even then, it is not a shortcut to myself but to wild images. Still, it's more alive than this surface life. Instant paradise in a plastic bag.

People who are experienced in meditation have discovered that they can indeed penetrate beneath surfaces without chemical means. Further, they can also discover not just disparate and ununified images but a *wholeness* to that powerful subsurface aliveness of which each of us is a part. What's more, they find that that sense of wholeness remains even after the "high" itself has passed. Gerard Manley Hopkins, the Jesuit poet, summed up what he saw of this inner life in a poem. To some, it could seem to be merely an ecological poem about man's indifferent destruction of the world. It is, however, intricate and revealing. In itself it is a fit subject for a meditation. Pore over it carefully line by line, not moving to the next line till you've absorbed this one.

God's Grandeur

The world is charged with the grandeur of God.
It will flame out, like shining from shook foil;
It gathers to a greatness, like the ooze of oil
Crushed. Why do men then now not reck* his rod?
Generations have trod, have trod, have trod;
And all is seared with trade; bleared, smeared with toil;
And wears man's smudge and shares man's smell: the soil
Is bare now, nor can foot feel, being shod.

And for all this**, nature is never spent;
There lives the dearest freshness deep down things;
And though the last lights off the black West went
Oh, morning, at the brown brink eastward, springs—
Because the Holy Ghost over the bent
World broods with wam breast and with ah! bright wings.

It is this "freshness deep down things" that we seek. We are not merely joined together by the impersonal atoms. We are joined to one another, to our

*Recognize his dominion.
**Despite all this.

universe, by a shared aliveness, like an underground spring of water from which everything draws its existence. That "freshness," that aliveness, that spring is the living God.

Halfway round the world from Hopkins and in a totally different culture, the same discovery was made along the same meditative path by the great modern Indian poet Rabindranath Tagore:

> The vitality that flows in waves,
> night and day through every vein of my body
> flows out to conquer the universe.
> It pulsates through the world
> in amazing rhythms and cadence;
> inspires every pore of the earth's soil
> with the thrill of a million grass-blades growing;
> blossoms into flowers and young leaves;
> sways, year after year,
> in the ceaseless ebb and flow
> of the undulating world-wide sea
> of life and death.***

This realization of the aliveness that pulses through me and through every living thing—and through God himself—at one time both liberates me from my tiny isolation and involves me "in the ceaseless ebb and flow of the undulating world-wide sea." Alone, I am limited; in union with this aliveness, I am limitless.

***Quoted by Johnston, *Christian Zen,* p. 101. Put into sense-lines by the present author.

Exercise

1. Relax. Let yourself go. Let go of all the problems and challenges of the world and its clocks and deadlines and expectations. Peace.

2. Let your breathing become regular, relaxed, slowed down. Concentrate your attention just on your own breathing, feeling it, absorbed in it. Imagine the air is something visible to your imagination, drawn in from outside, held and filling your body with oxygen, pumping the bellows of your lungs, feeding your heart and blood—and then exhaled, returned to our common atmosphere to be used by others. Repeat this consideration for as long as it keeps yielding up more and more: drawn in, working and being used, exhaled again.

3. Then let your imagination spread, understanding that this air you have used and passed on has been used by others in this place, in this town. Where did it come from? Whom has it sustained in life before you? Rest there, understanding, contemplating this truth of the air we all share.

4. The envelope of air encircles the globe, moving restlessly across its face, from Asia to California to Maine to Europe to Asia to California, in an endless return. It carries storms, rain, snow. It stirs the sands of the deserts and the waves of the sea. It wafts along pollen from plant to plant. The plants and trees absorb its carbon dioxide and give off oxygen to be breathed by animals and men, and in the process makes food for them to eat. It feeds fires. It is our common environment; we use it, pass it on, share it. Rest there, with your breathing

self at the focal point of this enlivening environment of air, breathing it in and out, in and out.

5. The Hebrew word for air or breath is *ruah*. It is the word Scripture uses not only for the atmosphere we breathe but also for the Holy Spirit. He is *the* living breath. Resting in the physical air you are breathing in and out, think of this wider scope of the breath that sustains us: the Spirit of God at creation hovering over the primeval waters "with warm breast and with ah! bright wings"; the Father fashioning Adam and "breathing into his nostrils a breath of life" which made him a living human being; the whirlwind and tongues of fire with which the Spirit of God visited the Apostles on Pentecost and made them alive with the aliveness of God.

6. Rest there in that life-giving air, breathing it into your lungs, drawing the Spirit into your self—surrounded by it, sustained by it, sharing it. Peaceful. Enlivened. Aware.

Wonder

If the last two meditations have given you some insight, you are quite likely at the edge of some real awareness of the presence of God within you and all around you. Most of us know *about* God, but very few of us know *God*. As a person, we can find out a certain amount about him from textbooks, just as textbooks and articles can yield a certain amount of information about any famous living person like Mick Jagger or Liz Taylor. But the information in a biography—or in the catechism or the Scriptures—is nothing at all compared to the actual experience of knowingly being in the person's immediate presence. Such "preliminary research for the interview" (which is about all most religious education attempts to do) is as necessary but ultimately disposable as the first stage of a moon rocket. At that point of real ignition, real encounter, the real Person takes over and makes all the written descriptions of him look like shadows.

Once one has personally encountered the Guest of Honor, Mass is no longer merely the same old deadly liturgical routine. A short passage of Scripture which describes Yahweh or his enfleshed Son is no longer the dry description of a stranger but of Someone we have encountered for ourselves. Even the "Our Father," which we piously rattled off as children with all the involvement of "two times two are four," now takes on a new life when it is slowly pondered phrase by phrase. It is no longer a matter of memory; it is a moment of meeting.

It seems inconceivable that this God of unutterable light, this Spirit of divine aliveness is within *me*, breathing, enlivening, divinizing me at the core of my humanity. And yet it is true. To ask why is a waste of time, just as it is a waste of time to ask why my friends love me. The fact is there; don't try to analyze it; revel in it! Enjoy it! Sing it! It is equally silly to analyze *how* this immeasurable God could permeate the whole universe and yet still be aware of me, focused into me. The fact is there; dance!

That does not mean that the fact of this divinely enlivening presence in and around me—like the

atoms and the air and the light—cannot be pondered. But it should be not something dissected with
the human reason but merely gazed at and enjoyed
by the human spirit—as all love must be. This is a
mystery to be wondered at, not a problem to be
solved. God is an infinite sea, and one can only float
blissfully on that sea and marvel at it. Trying to
"solve" it would be like trying to measure that sea
with a cup. Contemplating the life-giving presence of
God all around me is not a way to find answers; it is
a way to find joy.

Exercise

(This is a variation of the famous "Jesus
Prayer," which may be familiar to some
readers from J. D. Salinger's *Franny
and Zooey*.)

1. Relax. Let go of the world's busyness.
   Breathe deeply, hold it and let it out
   with a complete exhaustion of tension.
   Then gradually begin to regulate your
   breathing. Inhale for a count of five;
   exhale for a count of five. Try to make
   the counting gradually slower and
   slower until it is rhythmic and steady.
   Let it happen for awhile until you are
   comfortable with it and no longer have
   to count.
2. Then gradually and very quietly, as you
   inhale, say in the deepest part of yourself, "Jesus, son of my Father." On the
   exhale, say "Somehow you are alive in
   me." Do it over and over and over, resting in it, drawing aliveness and realization from it.
   It needn't be those words. As we will see
   later with the Zen *mantras*, the words
   are less important than the rhythm,

their ability to focus one's consciousness. But, unlike the Eastern contemplative, the Western mind is trained to demand some content, at least at the beginning of meditation. The reason I chose those words was that they mention Jesus, who is our link to the aliveness of the Father, whom he has shared with us. The second part could be any realization you have yourself and if, after a few repetitions, that phrase yields no results, change it to one of your own. There is an advantage, though, to the repetition of the same phrase, whatever it is. It is a place to come back to from distractions; the rhythm disconnects the discursive mind and releases the deeper faculties.

The purpose of this meditation is not to accumulate a whole rosary of insights but rather to establish a conscious contact through Jesus Christ with the alive presence of our common Father. Once you have achieved that, merely rest in that awareness. At that point the words can fall away into a silent sharing of aliveness with God.

Courage

Perhaps the greatest obstacle to people's continuing to pray is false expectations about what prayer is supposed to do, and the principal misapprehension is that its purpose is somehow to change God's mind. "Oh, God, please make me less weak, less prone to temptation!" Or, "Oh, God, don't let my mother die!" Or, "Oh, God, please end this war!" All of these begin to sound like attempts to remind a God, who has grown absent-minded in his old age, that we are in need of help. Sometimes such prayers even seem to presuppose a God who is a hard-hearted puppet-master manipulating every event in our lives, and we poor wretches come crawling to this sadist trying to make him more loving.

For whatever his reasons, God did create a universe in which evil was possible—both the physical evils of hurricanes and cancer and the moral evils that result from man's misuse of his free will. But our pitiable attempts to demand reasons for such a universe, from a God who is unanswerable to us, very subtly betray our ignorance or our unwillingness to accept "the way things are." They treat God as if he were just another man, superior to us no doubt, but nonetheless still on our level of being—like a very rich and famous man called by a poor and hard-done-by petitioner into a court where they both stood as equals before the bench. A little quiet thought shows the glaring weakness in that demand. It is not unlike the innocent arrogance of earlier men and women who thought that, because we are on it, all the planets must revolve around the Earth. Hard as that may be to accept, we are not the center of the universe, nor are we the center of Reality.

The kind of prayer that at least seems to be trying to get God to change his mind is not as reprehensible as I have made it sound. Moses prayed that his men might win battles; Martha prayed that Jesus would bring her brother back to life. And in the Garden of Gethsemane, the Best of Us begged his Father not to require him to go through the bloody slaughter that awaited him the next day. The difference, I think, is that all of those people knew what they were doing. They didn't expect or demand that things be changed. Their prayers were more like the outpourings of one friend to another friend who was no more capable of changing things than they themselves. When a friend pours out his sorrow to his friend at a wake, he is not expecting the friend to bring back the dead. He is merely drawing some sustenance and strength from sharing his sorrow with a friend who understands and loves and supports him with his presence.

God created someone to be an answer to your prayers, and that someone is you. Prayers like, "Oh, God, please help me pass this exam," and "Oh, God, help me not to be so mean to my mother," depend far more for their fulfillment on the person praying than on God. And they have far more likelihood of coming true if the pray-er realizes where the responsibility for their fulfillment truly lies, and that he has come to his Friend only to remind *himself* of what must be done.

Other petitionary prayers like, "Oh, God, please cure my father's cancer," are requests for things that are out of our hands and, in most cases, the result of the natural order of things, a complex of causes in which even God needn't be the principal influence at the moment. Such prayers are far less frustrating when we understand that here, too, we are merely asking for the courage to endure the results of the situation should they turn out to be painful. I think it is even worth picking our words carefully when we make such prayers of petition, so that we actually do recognize that we are really asking not for a miracle but for the support of a Friend, the continued awareness of his presence as we ourselves try to understand and cope with the suffering we are praying about.

As Louis Evely says very truly, every time we pray not for ourselves but for others, the proper effect of that prayer should be to make us do something for that person: write a letter, send a book, give a sign, make a phone call, do something—no matter what—so long as it is a visible sign, a kind of mini-sacrament. Such prayers are not so much reminders to God as reminders to oneself. C. S. Lewis put it well: it is far easier to pray for a boor than to go and visit him. When we ask God to take care of our parents, it should be like a man saying to his wife, "You know, I'm glad you put that idea into my head. I'm going to have to surprise Mom and Dad with a present."

The best teacher is one who does his job so well that he himself becomes no longer necessary. The same is true of God. He is best served when his children realize that they must not assume their Father's role in changing this world. It will be gradual; it will be imperfect; it will now be like a world where miracles are commonplace—unless we ourselves, as adult sons and daughters of our Father, become the miracle workers.

Be careful of what you ask of God. In truth, you are really asking it of yourself—and asking God to back you up while you do it. If you pray for the end of whatever war is currently in the news, you are really asking yourself to write a letter to your congressman.

Prayer is not a practical thing, in the sense that it is not an attempt to get things done as a direct result of the prayer, to change things outside oneself —including God's mind. It is, rather, an attempt to change things *inside* oneself: the weakness, the cowardice, the irritation or even rage at "the way things are," the inertia that keeps us from helping those in need or crying out against stupidity or injustice. The reason we pray is to realize, once again, that we are not alone, that we have the greatest of Friends always beside us—not to do our jobs for us, as a weaker father might do, but to support our courage to do our jobs for ourselves.

Prayer is, quite simply, presence and companionship. Just as all acts of love are.

Exercise

1. Go very calmly through one of the relaxation exercises, un-tensing your body, slowing down your breathing, putting your consciousness into a state of receptive peace. Verge into the presence of God.

2. Very, very slowly meditate on each phrase of the "Our Father"—even pausing and poring over it word by word. For instance, why is it "our" and not "my"? Aren't both true? What does it mean in the depth of myself? And so on. There is no need to move on to the next

word or phrase until the present one has
temporarily exhausted itself for you.
Don't be in a hurry. You don't have to
get through the whole prayer. If you
have given yourself fifteen minutes for
meditation, and you don't get past the
first word or two, it will have been a
truly fine prayer.

The purpose of this exercise is also to
consider, in each phrase, what you are
really asking of this Father of light and
air and aliveness and also what you are,
indeed, really asking of yourself.

Intimacy with God

The other principal obstacle to continued praying is one's fear that it is ineffectual—not in the
sense of changing God's mind but in the sense of my
not "getting anything out of it." In the first place,
achieving an ease at prayer takes time. But we've
been conditioned by the rush of the competitive
world, by the expectations of teachers and parents,
to feel guilty unless we "ransom the time," come up
with some concrete proof that we've really been
working. Also, we are perhaps preconditioned more
than we suspect by advertisements leading us to expect unconditional money-back guarantees for anything we have expended time or effort on.

Many people, especially beginners at prayer,
think the ten or fifteen minutes has been somehow
wasted if they don't come out the other end with
some great new insight or some brilliant new
rephrasing of an old insight or something to share
verbally with others. This is one reason I do not rec-

ommend keeping some kind of "prayer journal" as others do—unless of course a particular individual finds that it is actually helpful to him or her. Such logging of prayer experiences, in the first place, turns what should be a deepening realization of presence and companionship into something like a weight-watcher's regimen, always checking petty advances and petty failures. But what's more important, we do not subject our meetings with other friends to such appraisal after each encounter: "Did that work? Are we better friends than we were yesterday? Did I make any mistakes or progress?" Why should we do it with our attempts to get to know God better? It turns prayer into a Dale Carnegie class, with God as the potential customer to be won and influenced.

By allowing the fear of being ineffectual to enter into the state of prayer and by wishing to accomplish something myself, I spoil it all. It shows that *I* want to be in charge; *I* want to hurry this friendship along; *I* want to see results, and I want to see them damn quick, d'ya hear?

For some reason, what I have written reminds me of the cleaning lady who came into my room yesterday. She usually finds me typing away furiously at this machine. Yesterday, she found me just sitting here, staring into space, daydreaming, thinking. And she said, "Oh, you're not working today." Unless there is a noise, unless there is a tangible product, you are not really doing anything.

Such a beneath-the-surface Puritanism usually infects me on retreats. Over the course of eight days of sequential meditations in *The Spiritual Exercises*, one expects recognizable progress, new insights, deeper understanding. But one of the best retreats I have ever made—and I have made nearly thirty, two of them for a month each—was when I went alone to a cottage by a lake, and I said to myself, "I'm not going to make any progress. I'm not going to start at Meditation #1 and move inexorably to Meditation #2 and then #3. I'm just going to spend eight days with my Friend, like a husband and wife with a week away from the kids." And for eight days, the two of us did just that: took long walks together, talked a bit—mostly, alas, about me—but a large part of the time the two of us just sat silently together and watched the water and the trees and the sky. It wasn't the least bit "useful." I didn't "learn" anything I didn't know before. But it was peaceful, and it's good to spend time with your friend.

Prayer is not a time to seek ready-made answers; sometimes they do actually come, seemingly out of nowhere, but they can't be predicted or expected, much less demanded. What I seek is not answers but one particular realization: of a very real contact with the deepest part of myself and a merging of that deepest self into the rhythm, the light, the life of the living God, dwelling within me and all round me.

Come to prayer with no expectations. Be empty and expectant before him. It is not up to you to manufacture the light; all you have to do is open your self-protective shutters and raise the blinds. Those who approach prayer with their intelligence only seem almost to expect to "conquer God," like mastering the theory of relativity. But prayer is an opening of the self, making a place for him in your day and in your spirit, and calling God into that opening. When one does that, he finds that God was already there, waiting to be invited in.

Exercise

Prayer need not be a matter of words, though there is nothing wrong with words. Take a walk for ten or fifteen minutes in a place where you know you will not be too disturbed. Pause a minute before you begin and open yourself to God, acknowledge his presence—even with words like "Hello!" or "Hiya! I'm back again."

Then just set off on your walk as you would with any other good friend, tell him about your day as you would tell any friend who had gone through the day with you. "What did you think about . . . ?" And then pause, give him a chance to answer if he wants. Most often he won't. Like the best kind of friends he gets joy just listening to someone he loves prattle on and on. As with any good friend, knowing him, you can probably guess what he'd say anyway. But nonetheless we still ask. Stop when you feel like it and look—really look—at the things you pass. If there's no need to speak of it, merely look, conscious that he is looking at it with you and through you.

I need say nothing of how to end it. Who am I to tell two friends how to end a walk together?

CHOICE OR CHANCE?

Every year when I ask my senior theology students how they feel about prayer, the answers are varied but, almost without exception, each man says that he does actually pray sometimes. Also, almost everyone in the class says that he prays "sort of when I feel like it." I would guess that it is true of most nominal Christians that, outside Mass which is usually an uptight, mandated kind of prayer, they pray only "when the spirit moves me."

I wonder, though, if this is really the capital-"S" Spirit of God or the small-"s" spirit of human confusion and need. There's nothing wrong with praying from a desire to achieve some good or to avoid some suffering, but when that is the *only* time when "the spirit moves me," there is a strong basis for supposing that prayer means little more than panhandling. The only time I ever give God a second thought is when I am forced by some external pressure to go to Mass or when I'm forced to my knees by some inner problem that I can't solve alone.

Now God is not some doddering old miser who sits in his dark house, worth a grudging visit just in case the old fool will be willing to fork over this time. Nor does he sit there nursing hurt feelings because "The only time you visit me is when you want something!" Hard as it may be for some to admit, God doesn't need us—either our praise or our petitions or our thanksgiving. The point is that we need him, if we are to achieve the fullness of personhood of which we are capable. And we ought not waste any time worrying about God's hurt feelings about being ignored but rather consider what happens inside ourselves when we treat the Author of our lives as nothing more than a rare shoulder to cry on or an easy touch for a handout.

There are certain things in everybody's life that are considered essential: eating, sleeping, being with people, taking a shower. We all have to do those things, and we usually not only find time for them but usually do them at about the same time of the day. There are also things that we get done even when we feel down and out—feeding the baby, emptying the garbage, taking a tray up to someone sicker than we. If prayer is truly an essential part of our lives, not just a temporary fad, not just a time-killer like *The Edge of Night*, then it seems it should have a place set aside for it in our day, and we should make the small but definite decision about when it will be.

And prayer truly is essential for us, not only as humans but as Christians. As human beings we need time to regain our inner stability, time to re-collect the self—not the vague and surface "I" of everyday life but the real "I." And the solitude that prayer demands lets us face our true selves without all the posturing and pretense that helps us bluff our way through the day. When one is alone, he is not necessarily a better person, but he surely is more genuine.

As Christians, too, we need prayer. Without a real contact with the Person about whom the theology texts were written and whom the Mass celebrates, we are reading nothing more involving than the philosophical system of a dead rabbi and attending a meeting no more religious than a Kiwanis luncheon for a Guest of Honor who never shows up. One cannot remain a Christian very long without praying. Without it, we are no more than pagans with Christian labels.

Time

The people for whom prayer is a kind of accident turn to it only when they find themselves alone and in need. But there is a great difference between finding oneself alone and *putting* oneself alone, in order to recognize one's need for contact with the aliveness of God. As Jesus himself said, "When you pray, go into your room and close the door behind you."

There is no single answer to the question, "What time of day should I pray?" In a sense, there are as many answers to that question as there are readers of this book. Some find prayer easier in the morning when they are fresh; others don't really get all their circuits working till midmorning. Many find it easiest to pray at night when things have quieted down; others are just too bushed to focus their consciousness on anything more demanding than Johnny Carson. Each one has to find the best time for him and, among the times that are open in the day, experiment to discover which of those free times he or she finds most fruitful, easiest to relax attentively, easiest to make quiet contact with God.

As I have said before, there are certain areas of "fat" in the day which most of us have: riding to work or school, waiting outside offices, watching TV, talking on the phone, listening to records. Surely one of those unavoidable waits can be used to pray rather than merely to reread the subway ads for the tenth time. Surely we could spare ten or fifteen minutes out of the passive relaxations that we truly need—but rarely need for as long as we let them stretch on. Not to be crude, but one boy told me that he always prayed in the bathroom every morning and, to be sure, it is a time alone that none of us can avoid!

It is not at all important *when* we take the time; it is only important *that* we take the time—to acknowledge who we really are and with Whom we are truly united.

Place

The particular place is not important either, although most people who achieve an ease with meditation find that it is good to have one kind of "base" where they can be sure of some kind of solitude and silence for awhile. In a way, the ability to find someplace like that will condition what time of the day one chooses to meditate—when everyone is out of the house, when I have the office to myself, when the park isn't filled with kids and dogs. A great many people have no privacy where they live or work and therefore have to find their seclusion outside their familiar world, in a chapel, on a park bench, along a path in the woods. But surely each one of us can find some "secret place."

I have rarely been struck more forcefully by a picture of a film star than when I saw a photograph of Cicely Tyson sitting on a bench in a park, hands open and receptive on her lap, eyes cast down— praying. If someone as busy and "public" as she can find a place, surely so can I.

For many years I avoided praying in chapels because always, at the back of my mind, I would wonder if other people were coming in behind me, seeing me, saying to themselves, "How wonderfully pious he is!" In the first place, I didn't want to be considered pious, and in the second place I kept foolishly debating with myself whether I was sitting in the chapel only *because* I wanted to be seen and judged "good." Such idiocy was sure proof that my prayer at those times was not a letting go, not an opening up to God, but a focusing on myself—and only the surface self at that. For those fifteen minutes, who cares who sees you or what they think! If a chapel is the only place you can find solitude and quiet in your world, use it! Presumably the other visitors to the chapel are not there to keep watch on you; they are there for the same reason you are: to be alone with God.

The Body

The ironic thing about prayer is that the whole person has to be both relaxed and at the same time attentive. Our bodies are the major sources of distraction from achieving this quiet receptivity. They itch, they gurgle, they cramp, they tense up. They are lured out of concentration by the slightest sounds. The *Bhagavad-Gita*, the Hindu scriptures, say that the stillness of the mind in meditation should be like a candle flame in a windless place— but we live in a world where drafts come from the most unexpected places. As a result, many modern books on prayer spend a great deal of time trying to appropriate the methods of Eastern body control in order to lessen distractions and focus the attention of those who meditate.

As with choosing a time and place for prayer, choosing a position which is most conducive to prayer is a matter of individual experiment. Even within a single prayer period, the position may be altered as the body either gets in the way of concentration or, in more experienced meditators, moves naturally into a position that embodies the mood of the prayer. For instance, when someone is praying and begins to feel a sense of profound awe at the presence of God, he may move from a sitting position to kneeling, even with his face to the floor (Figure 1).

Figure 1

To Westerners who are painfully uptight about body movements (except at rock concerts), the infinite ways that the body can express inner spiritual states and even enhance them is severely limited. But if one is alone in his room, why should he worry who "sees" him?

In general, however, one should find a kind of "rest" position in which he begins his prayer and remain there, even if it takes a kind of quiet self-discipline. (In Zen prayer halls, there is a monk with a willowy stick who comes along and gives you a good sharp thwap if you become fidgety!) The urge to get up and walk around is often a sign that the person is getting itchy, that the prayer is not being "effectual," that nothing is "happening." Controlling the urge to get up and move very often is the threshold of a real inner breakthrough. Therefore, without making a big deal about bodily posture, it is worthwhile to find one or two basic "rest" positions that help you personally and stick with them, especially at the beginning.

Kneeling is the most traditional and obvious Western posture at prayer but, as many a novice can testify, kneeling can be a distraction in itself, focusing all one's attention not on the God who dwells within him but on his aching knees. If it helps to symbolize your inner feelings at the time, use it; if not, there are many other possible prayerful positions.

Lying flat on your back is probably the most restful posture for prayer, but it has one drawback: you often fall asleep.

Sitting is perhaps the best position in which to pray, for most people. One can relax but at the same time be attentive and "focused." The sitting position already described in the exercises is simply sitting in a straight chair, head tilted slightly forward or backward, hands resting on the lap or on the knees (Figure 4). But the masters of Zen meditation are quite

Figure 4

convinced that the lotus posture somehow "organizes" the whole body—breathing, movement of the blood, even the composition of the body fluids—

to such an extent that the whole body is under control, nonintrusive, at peace. The great difficulty about the lotus is that Westerners, unused to sitting without support, find at least the full lotus as difficult to sustain and as distracting as kneeling.

In the full lotus (Figures 2 and 3), one sits on

Figure 2   *Figure 3*

the edge of a pillow or cushion, knees widespread, feet crossed at the calves and each foot resting on the crook of the opposite knee. (That's the hard part!) The hands rest on the heels of the feet, fingers resting on one another, thumbs slightly touching to make the hands a little circle.

A variation of this, the half-lotus, is little different from sitting cross-legged, Indian-style. For those unwilling or unable to endure the practice it takes to be comfortable and undistracted by cricks and cramps in the full lotus, sitting Indian-style, back relatively straight, is comfortable and yet not comfortable enough to let one fall asleep.

In his book, *Christian Zen*, William Johnston says,

The lotus position somehow impedes discursive reasoning and thinking; it somehow checks the stream of consciousness that flows across the surface of the mind; it detaches one from the very process of thinking. Probably it is the worst position for philosophizing but the best for going down, down to the center of one's being in imageless and silent contemplation.

The important thing to remember about posture in prayer is that it should be comfortable enough to eliminate distractions but not so comfortable as lounging. Prayer should be a time when one is at ease but not so at ease as to be "all over the place." Too much sprawling during prayer destroys the concentration of one's full consciousness.

As I have tried to emphasize in the meditation exercises, control of breathing can be very helpful in putting the body and therefore the mind into a state of peace that frees the spirit from both body and mind. Every period of prayer should begin with some kind of conscious exercise to withdraw oneself from the daily fuss and rush, to focus on the person—your self—whom you are offering to unite with the divine presence who dwells within you. One way of getting "into" your self is to begin by focusing on your own breathing.

It takes more than a little practice to be able to sit and meditate, as Zen monks do, with the eyes open. I personally still cannot do it except at very special times, like near water or by a fire or when the sky is ablaze with stars. In a way, the eyes are

the hungriest of our senses, and they insist on dart-
ing about, taking everything in. This curiosity is ad-
mirable most of the time, but when one is trying to
focus all his powers *inside* himself, they can be a
powerful distraction. Even Buddhists who can meditate open-eyed usually focus their eyes on a crack in
the floor or a spot on the wall and lock it there till
the spot has no new evidence, no unexplored aspects
that could lead the mind away.

Another means they use is the *mandala*, some
physical object with symbolic value that focuses the
attention. They realize that, once the eyes begin to
wander, you are lost. Some Christians use a crucifix
as a *mandala*, holding it lightly in their laps and
focusing their attention *into* it and what it means. In
most modern churches, for liturgical reasons, to
make the altar the center of attention, the tabernacle
with its flickering red lamp has been moved to one
side. This is fine, I suppose, for the majority of
Christians whose only time for prayer is an hour on
Sunday, but a regrettable loss of one more *mandala*
for the smaller number of Christians who like to
drop into a church and pray more often than once a
week.

A Director

Beginners who are serious about prayer, who
want to pray by choice and not by chance, really
should seek out some wise man or woman to advise
them about their prayer. The most obvious advantage of having a director is having the chance to talk
unabashedly about prayer to someone who not only

understands its importance to you but who prays himself. It's nice to know that you're not the only one trying to grow in prayer, that it's really an important part of others' lives, too.

Having a director is also a good source of new ideas, new ways to relax and to focus one's consciousness. But it's also good to have someone you talk to once a month or so about what progress you are making, what seems to be getting in the way. Talking every few weeks with another pray-er seems to be far better and less check-listy and self-centered than a kind of "prayer journal," and an advisor can not only keep you at it but also give you a kick in the pants when you're becoming insufferably pious or overly serious.

If praying makes you an old stick-in-the-mud, you're surely doing something wrong. When prayer is true and honest and really in touch with the aliveness of God, it should not be cramping but liberating. The people I know who pray the best seem able to spread a quiet joy wherever they go. And why not? The aliveness of God should be the most joyful infection around!

SOME METHODS OF PRAYING

No matter what our age, sex, color, all human beings have certain needs and hopes and vices in common. At the same time, though, no two of us has precisely the same tastes and susceptibilities. Therefore, in a book like this, it is impossible to suggest the one sure-fire method of meditating that can be used by every man and woman with a money-back guarantee. Therefore, I offer the few methods I know of—there are many, many more—in the hopes that one or two may prove useful or at the very least inspire the reader to seek wiser sources than myself.

Also, some methods of praying work very well for awhile and then start to wither away. It is helpful to have other methods to fall back on both when the method you're presently using ceases to be fruitful and when your mood calls for something different in order to "prime the pump."

Genuine prayer always has some constants, though: the deliberate withdrawal into solitude from the cares and hurry of the day, the active attempt to focus one's consciousness, and the awareness of being in the presence of the Other, the living God. But the methods, the content, the communication itself will vary from person to person, from occasion to occasion.

The Mantra

Transcendental Meditation (TM) has adapted some of the methods of Eastern mysticism, not necessarily to help people pray but merely, on the human level, to achieve some peace and to marshal the consciousness to live and work more effectively and with a greater sense of fulfillment. After exercises in relaxation, in regulating the breathing, and in concentrating the consciousness, the student is given a mantra, usually in Sanskrit, the meaning of which he or she is completely ignorant of. The meaning of the words is not as important as the rhythms, the way the constant and peaceful repetition of the sound limits the rational consciousness to *one* process: achieving a kind of "one-pointedness." In so doing, it opens up the unused power of the mind and spirit into an area of the self that is ordinarily dormant.

Mantras are a simple form of achieving peace. They are also a good guard against distraction—like the tangible mandala—and something to return to if the attention has wandered off. The sheer boredom that repetition induces in the logical mind forces the consciousness downward—almost like the hypnotic effect of watching flames in a fireplace or listening to the drumming of the rain. It almost inevitably makes one meditative.

The most famous mantra is "OM," which the subject repeats over and over, feeling the vibrations in his mouth and head and whole body, yielding to the sound. "The Jesus Prayer" mentioned before is a kind of Christian mantra, and when it is done right, so is the rosary—which is not only a Christian practice but a Buddhist one as well.

After the usual relaxation exercises and the quieting of the senses, repeat a single word—"Jesus" or "Father" or "love"—very quietly and calmly over and over and over, feeling the vibrations and the rhythms. I find that when I am distracted, the word "OM" can almost always bring me back to a point of peaceful focus. Try it.

The Koan

Many poems, many parts of Scripture are so cryptic that we read them once, presume they are "meaningless for me," and pass on. We have been conditioned by the easy-access pabulum of TV to expect that anything worth hearing or reading has to be in words that any backward three-year old could understand. We have also been conditioned by our education to expect that a teacher will explain anything murky *for* us so that we need never figure out anything for ourselves. Thus we impoverish ourselves.

The Eastern mystics, however, have taken the precisely opposite tack. One of their methods is the koan, a seemingly unanswerable riddle that the Zen master gives his student and tells him to pore over it hour after hour after hour. The most famous one is,

"We know the sound of two hands clapping, but what is the sound of one hand clapping?" And, oddly, the focusing of consciousness, the intensity of quiet concentration, the prolonged dedication suddenly causes the persistent monk to burst through into "enlightenment." Basically, the koan is a gimmick to frustrate the mind at its upper level of discursive, rationalizing logic and thus force it to break through, down into a deeper level of psychic activity.

After the usual relaxation exercise, focus all your attention on *one* of the many such seemingly impossible statements of the Scriptures:

> —"The innocent suffer while the wicked man prospers."
> —"Sell all you have, give to the poor, and come follow me."
> —"This is my Body."
> —"He must increase; I must decrease."
> —"I live now—not I, but Christ lives in me."

One way is to begin with a mantra, like "Jesus" or "My Father," and establish it as a kind of bass rhythm to one's prayer. Then, with that basic rhythm regularized with one's breathing and whole inner self, turn the attention to the statement of the koan and ponder it, weigh it, roll it around in your mind against the rhythmic background of the mantra.

Remember: you are not trying to figure it out logically, like a riddle or a math problem. Those one-sentence, apparently impossible statements from the Scripture are—like our physical, surface bodies

—only the tip of the iceberg. For instance, when someone you have loved for a long time suddenly says, "You know what? I really love you," there is a whole universe of meanings behind those words. Compared to the host of meanings they contain, the words and sounds that carry the meanings are as thin and unsubstantial as husks. And when you sit and ponder those words—"I love you"—echoing in the back of your mind in the voice of someone you love, you do not list the meanings or count them or sort them out logically. You immerse yourself in them, moving intuitively and joyfully from one into the other and back again. And while you are reveling in those unnumbered beautiful meanings, there is no awareness of time or place or distraction.

Try hearing God say the same thing to you: I love you.

Hard to believe, huh? And yet, impossibly, it's true.

Scripture: Pondering Ideas

Many people are turned off by the Scriptures because they seem so impenetrable. Very often this is caused by taking too much at one bite. Other times we are hampered by doubts, "Was there really a star to guide the Magi?" Or by stupid questions, "Did Adam have a navel?" Or by using the Scriptures to prove or attack the claims of Christianity, "If Jesus actually walked on water, then how come . . . ?" Forget all the complications and let the words enter your guts where they can begin to live. As William Johnston says, "Let them live at the psychedelic level. Get the kick those Semitic writers are trying to give you. Then you'll find the scriptures are food and that they are life."*

Sit down with the Scriptures in your lap. Relax, pull away from the world and center your consciousness on the inner powers deep inside you. Then open the Scriptures anyplace and begin to focus that inner power on God's elusive communication through the words on the page. Just be sure to make the section small, no more than four or five verses. Some people like to start, say, at the beginning of an Epistle of Paul and move gradually, day by day, through it. Whether you open at random or work steadily through from part to part, the important thing is to take small bites, only four or five lines at a time. Rest in them, savor them as you did the koan: "What are these strange words trying to say to *me*?" There is no need to "get through" or "knock off" another Epistle or Gospel. *Non multa sed multum.*

If you are unfamiliar or uneasy with Scripture, try one of these to start:

—Isaiah, 6:6-8
—Matthew, 25:37-40
—Mark, 8:31-33
—Luke, 14:12-14
—John, 1:1-5, 9-14

—Romans, 7:4-6
—I Corinthians, 13:8-13
—Ephesians, 3:14-19
—Philippians, 2:5-11
—Hebrews, 5:1-4

If it helps, picture yourself as a prophet or evangelist or Epistle writer, who feels the inner stirrings of this message from God for the very first time. "And the word of God came to me saying. . . ." What does it mean? Why is he saying this to *me*?

*Christian Zen, p. 65.

Controlled Daydreaming

There is a difference between mulling over the ideas of the Scriptures and reliving the Scriptures in your imagination. Ideas still have some relationship to the discursive, reasoning intelligence and because most of us are more used to working on that level, I treated ideas first. They are the kinds of mental activities one associates in school with nonfiction: essays, discussions, lectures, probing ideas from many different angles. And, indeed, there is much of the Scripture that concerns itself with handling truth in that mode.

But the Scriptures are not only the repository of the ideas of Jesus, they are also a story about a Person. Not only were the words he spoke a revelation of the Good News, but his actions were also revelatory. Therefore, one can not only mull over his ideas but can also learn from trying in the imagination to relive the Gospel story. However, we are much more conditioned by our education to discuss and debate ideas than to relive a story in our imaginations.

When I was a kid, I remember lying on the floor for an hour every evening listening to our old Sonora radio spew out the adventures of Captain Midnight and Jack Armstrong, the Shadow and the Green Hornet. They were real to me, alive. They were not just men and women standing in street clothes at microphones in some faraway studio; this was really an on-the-spot broadcast from the jungle at the headwaters of the Orinoco, and Jack and Billy and Betty were exuding real sweat as they squatted in real muck to escape the vicious Auca Indians. My imagination took those sounds and built a world out of them, sometimes more real than the radio itself or the carpet I was sprawled on.

It must have been easier to recreate new worlds with one's imagination in the cold stone dining halls of medieval castles as a minstrel spun out the tales of Arthur and Beowulf for the enraptured. It must have been easier to visualize the story of the Gospels in the dank darkness of the catacombs. For most of the world's history, words alone were enough for strong imaginations to summon up the actual places and persons in any story. But today, most of our visualization is done for us. We needn't imagine what Mister Spock's face looks like as the Klingons creep toward him across the rocks of some nameless planet. It's right there, done for us by Leonard Nimoy, his make-up artist and their director. The only job the imagination is called on to do is lull us into a state of suspended disbelief that these are merely impulses on the flat surface of a cathode ray tube, that Marshal Dillon is not really inside that little box. Children still have some vestige of real-ization left; some of them wonder when Mommy is going to dust out all those dead Indians from the floor inside the TV set. But they get over that quickly.

Most of us still daydream once in awhile, letting our imaginations lure us out into situations that never were and never will be. At least in adolescence, the erotic passages of a novel can stimulate the imagination to visualize the scene—all the sounds, the textures, the pounding hearts. But even then, it has to be pretty steamy to capture our imaginations, gone limp and rubbery from so many prefab images in films and television.

It was probably easier to pray in the days before the mass media assumed our powers of thinking and visualizing. Not only were there fewer distractions then, not only were there fewer passive entertainments with which to wile away the empty hours, but that very lack of prefab images made the individual's imagination work far more, strengthen itself, reach. An audience looking at Shakespeare's nearly barren stage was forced to visualize its own bushes and trees and spangled skies—with little more than Shakespeare's poetry to evoke it from the rich wells of their own imaginations and from sense-memories more sensitized than ours.

The person who brings a well-stocked and sensitive imagination to prayer has a great deal more going for him than one who has let most of his visualization be done for him. He is, after all, trying to contact a way of existing and a Person that can never be adequately concretized. The God we pray to has revealed himself to have numberless facets— love, anger, mercy, justice; he made a world out of nothing and turned death into a doorway to newer life. To cope with such a mercurial Being takes a person capable of keeping all sorts of colored balls spinning in the air at once. We are all, in a sense, *les jongleurs de Dieu* when we pray.

It seems wise to me, therefore, to offer a few

limbering-up exercises for those who feel that their imaginations have sagged and are unable to tap the rich source of energy that lurks below the surface mind, a source of creative power that can make the Scriptures come alive and real-ized.

(1) In all these exercises, do a preliminary relaxation to clear the senses of stimuli actually working on you at the moment. Try to focus all your powers on recreating the sense-memory of the object called for. In the case of each sense, the objects become more and more subtle and therefore more and more difficult to recreate, to real-ize.

Taste: First try to recreate in your memory and imagination the taste of garlic. Feel what it does to your tongue, the roof of your mouth, your throat, your nose. Don't move to the next one until you've "got" garlic in your mouth. Then try Dentyne chewing gum. Again, be sure you have the taste before going on. Then, a chocolate bar. Since all the senses work together, include in the taste the sound of the paper ripping, the texture and sound of the foil, the movement of your teeth and tongue as you chew the candy. Then strawberry ice cream. Then margarine.

Texture: The rough bark of a tree . . . burlap . . . silk or nylon . . . a pile of dry leaves . . . pudding. Again, you feel not only with your hands but your cheeks and your feet. Make the re-creation as real as you can.

Movement: Here, too, feel the sensations not only in your hands but in all your muscles, your back, your legs, the blood in your head: jumping on a trampoline . . . rowing a small boat in choppy waters . . . walking in knee-deep water by a lake or along a creek . . . running on wet pavement . . . standing at attention in the hot sun.

Sound: Re-experience the moment not only with your ears but with the reactions that the sounds set up in the pit of your stomach, on the hairs at the back of your neck: a crack of thunder at night and its receding rumblings . . . crackling of flames . . . water poured onto the ashes of a fire . . . a single pair of footsteps on a dark street . . . an empty classroom at night.

Sight: A flash of lightning on a stormy night . . . a sunset over water or behind hills or buildings . . . catsup on a greasy hamburger . . . the surface of a cup of coffee . . . sunlight on a window sill.

(2) Now try to focus all your sense-memories on a single object—a piece of plain white bread, a stalk of crisp green celery, a peppermint Life-Saver. Choose just one. In your imagination, pick it up, feel its textures, bring it right up to your nose and sniff its fragrance. Put it in your mouth and feel the muscles working, hear the sound they make working together. Then try to sum up the whole experience as if it were happening right now.

(3) Now use all the senses, step by step, on a more extended scene—a stormy night alone in a hilltop cabin, riding the subway at night, a hot afternoon at the beach. Let your imagination move from object to object, from moment to moment, as if you were right there. Even though you've never been in such a place at such a time, your imagination can

take you there. Stored up in your sense-memories are all the tastes and smells and colors and sounds and textures and muscle movements of your past, and from them you can fabricate a situation that has never really happened to you.

Obviously these exercises couldn't be called prayer, although they could lead to it. They truly are an attempt to pull out of the rat race in which we rush heedlessly past most of the objects of God's creation, gobbling, skimming, half-hearing, half-seeing. In that sense, it is truly a tribute to the Artist of such an infinitely faceted creation that we pause and savor and give praise to his work.

Scripture: Inner Visualization

One of the reasons so few people get enjoyment out of reading literature—especially plays—is that they have not trained themselves to visualize inside themselves what is actually going on. The same is true of reading Scripture. Our minds are so clotted with the witless attempts Hollywood has made at embodying the story of the New Testament and with the ugly plaster statues that clutter our churches and schools and dashboards that we rarely make the effort to visualize for ourselves our own Jesus, Mary, Nicodemus, Judas. More than one period of meditation could be filled merely trying to conjure up for oneself what Jesus really looked like as if *you* were casting the movie: his flesh color, his hair, his face, his body. Don't settle for a plastic stereotype; make him real. Another way to approach it: how would he look if he lived today? What kind of clothes would he wear? As in the last exercise, use all your senses to summon him up.

What you are looking for is an inner visualization, using all your knowledge and all your sense-memories of sight and touch and taste and smell to recreate for yourself an event of the Gospels. Feel free in the scene, be part of it—either as one of the participants or as some anonymous passer-by. Run your hands over the rough textures of the animals at the nativity. Feel your nose and throat and toes clotted with the dust as Jesus walks along the roads with his friends. Hear the clang of the hammers and the jeers of the crowd and the thud of the cross as it falls into the hole on the hill of Calvary. Just pick the event—any event in the Gospels—and *be* there.

One method of doing this I stumbled on during my retreat this year. I was having a very dry time of it, four or five hour-long meditations each day, and when I came to the episode of Jesus washing the disciples' feet, I came to what seemed to be a dead standstill. I couldn't visualize it at all; I couldn't even get started. They were all the pasteboard stereotypes of cheap holy cards, not human beings. My wise director, knowing that such times are the sign one is getting close to a breakthrough, told me, "Okay, do it again." I ground my teeth, but I tried it again. But this time, instead of merely trying to visualize the scene out of thin air or even from remembered pictures of Jews in *The National Geographic*, I decided I'd try to visualize around the table of the Last Supper not the apostles of holy pictures but

Jesuits of my own community in Rochester. Suddenly that scene had a whole new reality and a whole new meaning for me that it had never had before. I could see individuals reacting to Jesus' actions not as pasteboard, one-dimensional characters but as men I'd known and lived with for years. As Jesus moved from one of us to the next and said, "Just as I'm washing your feet, you must wash one another's feet," I could hear us saying inside ourselves, "Well, I'll wash his feet. And I'll wash his feet. But I'll be damned if I'll wash *his* feet!" These men were no longer the goody-goody apostles of Hollywood movies; they were human beings reacting to this surprising Person.

Choose any event, read the Scripture passage slowly, and then put the book aside. Begin at the very beginning and be there, sense-memories alive and probing, and move step by step with people you know. One of the most readily accessible scenes is the Passion. Put yourself in Jesus' place. Feel the wood on your shoulders, the spittle in your face, the raw flesh on your back, the blows, the crush of bodies. Smell the sweat, the stink of breath, the sour wine, the dust. Step by step.

The next time you see a crucifix it will look different.

PRAYER WHEN YOU DON'T FEEL LIKE PRAYING

Very few people run around all day mumbling the name of Jesus. There are a thousand events and people that clutter our waking hours, demand our time and attention and energy. Very honestly, there are times when—even if we have a deep conviction that we want to pray at least a bit every day—the spirit is willing but the flesh is not only weak but digs in its heels and resists. You can plunk yourself grumblingly down into a perfect lotus and grit your teeth as you face the intimidatingly blank wall, and the spirit inside you just seethes with restlessness. No problem. That's the time to realize that no one is perfect, no one can achieve peace and contact with his deep self every day of the year.

But it needn't be a day without some kind of prayer; it's just a day for prayer of a different kind. There are far more possibilities than I outline here, but I offer these for a rainy day, some of them "doing" prayers, some of them remembering prayers

94

—which are more discursive than the kind of prayer we have considered so far.

Rewriting Scripture

Meditating on Scripture, in the real sense, means merely letting the meaning of a short passage seep into you, as we have seen. But at moments when the old devil of progress demands some kind of visible results, some kind of physical movement, one way to thwart him is to compromise with your mood instead of foregoing prayer completely. Anyone who has rambled through the Scriptures has a favorite Psalm or a favorite paragraph of the Gospels that has always "talked" to him or her, even though it seems as dull as dust on this particular day.

Get yourself a few sheets of paper and open to the passage of Scripture and start, line by line, translating it into words and images that are meaningful to you. Try as much as you can to realize that the Author of Scripture is sitting there beside you, interested, making suggestions, understanding very well that although you can't pray for a long stretch today you're pondering his words and trying to assimilate them as well as you can at the moment.

In a book called *God Is for Real, Man!* the chaplain of the Buffalo city jail gives the results of what his juvenile delinquent classes did to the Scriptures. For instance, one boy took Psalm 23 ("The Lord is my shepherd . . ."). Now, to a street-tough kid, the image of a gentle keeper of sheep is utterly without content. So he came up with, "The Lord is my probation officer . . ." using the best image he could find of a truly kindly and protective leader who was willing to sacrifice himself to keep the boy out of trouble. More cautious people might think this disrespectful. But in the first place the Scriptures were intended to communicate the truth not just to literary purists but to all men and women and children. In the second place even Paul says that the Spirit of Jesus within us enables us to call God "Abba." Now to a Jew, "Abba" did not mean "Eminent Sir" or "Divine Parent" or anything really classy like that. It did not mean even "Father." It meant "Papa" or "Dad." So much for the purists.

Here is one I did on a doldrummy day on Psalm 8. It was enough to keep me going for a couple of days of a dry-as-dust mood. Now that I've written it out, I can go back at times and slowly, prayerfully use it again, because it is *my* psalm now as much as it is the original psalmist's.

OH GOD, MY GOD.
How utterly your presence fills all the earth!
The stars sing your glory
    back and forth across the night sky.
You have made the wide-eyed children and their wonder
    to be your great surprise
    for the learned
    for the sophisticated
    for the cynical.

When I look up at the vast heavens
    the moon and the stars that you made
with your fingers

and set spinning through endless ages of
space and time,

I wonder at you.

What is mankind
　　that you care so much for us,
　　that in this steady and loyal universe
　　　　you chose such changeable creatures
as us?

　　You made us only a little less than yourself.
　　You have crowned us with glory and
honor.
　　You have taken all that your hands have
made
　　　　and given us the lordship over it—
　　　　　　darkness and light,
　　　　　　waters and sky,
　　　　　　plants and trees and their seed,
　　　　　　the fish of the sea,
　　　　　　the birds of the air
　　　　　　and the beasts of the field,

　　　　because, of all your creatures, only we
　　　　are made in your image and likeness.

What is man, that you care so much for us?

OH GOD, MY GOD!

How utterly your presence fills all the
earth!

And here is one from the New Testament, an
attempt to rewrite the first three Beatitudes—not to
tamper with the Gospels but to make them say
something to me when the words I had been accus-

tomed to for so many readings didn't seem to say anything any more:

> How lucky you are when your spirit's hungry; then you'll go out and find what will fill it: the kingdom of heaven.

> How lucky you are when you're in need of comforting; then you'll realize how much you need one another . . . and your Father.

> How lucky you are when you're gentle and willing to be taken in; then all the earth is open to you.

I've given only three here. But if on a particular day you feel that you have to do-pray rather than do-nothing-pray, open the Gospel of Matthew, chapter 5, verses 3 to 12, and see what you can do along the same line. Remember, you don't have to finish them all. If you do one for the whole fifteen minutes, that's just fine and dandy!

Composing Prayers

When worse comes to worst, one way to pray when you want to but don't feel up to it is writing the prayer out. Sort of like a short letter to God when he seems farther away than usual. It's a very honorable way to pray—after all, if the psalmists never wrote their prayers down, we'd never have them now. There is only one caution I would make about prayers one writes out. Most such prayers, once they're written, should be ripped up and thrown away. Otherwise, prayer could become something "useful," something with a physical product. Also, when the prayer is going to be filed away someplace, one tends to begin fussing over pretty phraseology, when really the whole purpose of prayer should be a spontaneous sharing of one's presence and aliveness, with no care about misplaced modifiers and spelling.

Some prayers you may want to keep, though. They are sometimes helpful when you are in the same kind of mood later on, triggering a more meditative kind of prayer all over again at a later date.

Here is one St. Augustine obviously decided was not only worth keeping but worth sharing:

MY GOD,

What is it that I love when I love you?

Not the beauty of any bodily thing
    nor the order of the seasons,
    nor the brightness of light that rejoices
the eye,
    nor the sweet melodies of all songs,
    nor the fragrance of flowers and oint-
ments and spices,
    nor manna nor honey,
    nor limbs that carnal love embraces.

None of these things do I love when I love
my God.

Yet
in a sense
I do love light
    and melody

and fragrance
and food
and embrace,

when I love my God.

The light
and the voice
and the food
and the fragrance
and the embrace in the soul

when the light shines upon my soul
which no place can contain,

when that voice sounds
which no time can take away,

I breathe a fragrance
which no wind scatters;

I eat a food
which is not lessened by the eating;

And I lie in an embrace
which satiety never comes to sunder.

This is what I love

when I love my God.

In his novel *Helena*, Evelyn Waugh composed this prayer and put it on the lips of the saintly mother of the Emperor Constantine. It is a prayer to the Magi—learned, rich men like the Empress herself, who seem to find small encouragement in a Kingdom of God that shows such a strong predilection for the poor:

Like me, you were late in coming.
For you the primordial discipline
    of the heavens was relaxed
    and a new defiant light blazed
    amid the disconcerted stars.
How laboriously you came
    taking sights and calculating.
How odd you looked on the road
    laden with such preposterous gifts.
Yet you came, and were not turned away.
Your gifts were not needed,
But they were accepted and put carefully
by,
For they were brought with love.

Dear Cousins, pray for me,
for his sake
Who did not reject your curious gifts.

Pray always for all the learned,
    the oblique, the delicate.
Let them not be quite forgotten
At the throne of God
When the simple come into their kingdom.

Finally, here is one I wrote myself, God knows
when, which more or less sums up the mood one is in
when he resorts to writing prayers rather than meditating:

DEAR GOD

I'm surrounded by 'shoulds'—
    "When are you going to . . .?"
    "You really ought to . . ."
    "There's not much time left."

My desk is a disaster area.

There are letters unanswered,
    and assignments ungraded,
    and unread books.

It makes a hollow fear in my belly
    to realize
        all the empty places still in my life,
        all the promises I've made,
        all the deadlines I've agreed to,
        all that 'they' expect of me,
        all the things that, because
            I love them
            and you
            and my life,

        I should do soon
        —or sooner.

There is so much to do, and so little time.

They are all, each in its way, important.

But because you are the reason
    and the cause
    and the aliveness

    of all I have left to do,

Give me the wisdom to set aside this page
    and be with you.

But in general, such prayers should be thrown away—in a sense, "sent," so that their purpose is to communicate with God, not to set up a stockpile of prayers that I can later con someone else into reading or publishing. Except for the best of them, written prayers should be just between my Friend and me.

Walking Prayers

I could just as well have entitled this "waiting-room prayers" or "driving-the-car prayers." There are times in the day when one is occupied-but-not-occupied: waiting for the dentist, driving along the freeway, hustling along the street from one place to another. There are distractions available with which to kill time: the Musak, the car radio, the shop window, the back-issue magazines on the waiting-room tables. But one could just as well use some of the time to find a little pocket of peace, to renew the awareness of the divine aliveness he holds at the depths of his being. (I am not saying that one has to pack every spare moment with praying, only that it is one of the many things one is free to do at that time.)

There are also times when one is too itchy to sit and meditate, times when there is not even the patience to sit and write prayers, times when you just have to get the roof off your head. No problem. Just get out and start walking in the woods or in a park or even along a city street. But as you begin, focus your consciousness on your Companion. You are not just going for a walk to "figure things out" or "clear your head." You are going for a walk with a Companion.

The People I Love

The prayer I find easiest while I'm driving is to focus my attention, one by one, on the people I love and who love me. It is not some quantitative struggle to fill up some kind of mental photo album. It is merely allowing each one of these people to rise up into your consciousness, see their faces, ponder how much they mean to you, remember trials and joys you've shared, and then thank God for allowing that person to exist and to be known and loved.

Don't rush on to the next one, like "God bless Mommy and Daddy and Uncle Fred and. . . ." Let each person stay at the center of your attention, your one-pointedness, for as long as they will. Then let another take over. Savor them. Be grateful for them. And then association will lead you to another and another.

If you are as lucky as I am—and you probably are—you can drive or walk for a full hour with those friends and wonder where the time has gone. But I am certain that when you get where you are going, you will have joy. You will realize how truly fortunate you are, and there will be no difficulty in praising and thanking the Giver of so many good gifts.

A Lifetime

Another method of slightly structured prayer is to think back to the first thing you can remember—a toy, a snowfall, a playmate—and, as with the persons you have loved, move gradually through the years from event to event, from person to person, savoring, reassessing, expressing gratitude not only for the joyous moments but also for the painful ones, which have left you wiser than before.

If you are praying in the evening or in the late afternoon, you can do the same thing with your day, beginning from the first moment you began to come awake and be aware. Realize what a great moment that is—waking up to a new day—a gift that we take so much for granted most of our lives. There is no rule that says you have to wake up every morning; there is a morning somewhere in your future when you won't wake up. So this morning was just one more gift. Then move slowly through the events of the day from that first moment until now, not like a kind of "examination of conscience" but more as an examination of consciousness. There will be events in the day you will regret; fine, you've realized it at least, and tomorrow you can do something about it. But the main attention should merely be on going over your day with a Friend who gave it to you and lived through it with you. Your day then becomes not just a disconnected series of events you have gone through but a whole, something you have summed up and possess.

Chance

Another kind of prayer that is sometimes even a bit of fun is to ponder the endless numbers of lucky chances that have enriched your life. (Chance, or design?) I think sometimes, what if my parents had never met? What if my dad, who was a truck driver, had not stopped into the store where my mother worked? What if he'd been too shy to ask for a date? What if they'd said, "One child is enough." My mother lost three or four babies in miscarriages between my sister and myself; why not me? Children are born deaf and blind, retarded, unwanted, battered; why not me? At one time the people I love most were total strangers; what happened that they should have become so precious, so essential to my life?

Of course there are no answers to those questions. And one can say, "Well, if such-and-such had never happened, I'd be none the wiser, would I?" But the fact is that such-and-such *did* happen, and the joy they have given me is something I did nothing to deserve. I have to be grateful to Someone! And gratitude is prayer indeed.

TRANSFORMING PRAYERS

If our eyes and ears are sensitized enough, God speaks to us in all kinds of ways, not merely through the Scriptures and through nature. He speaks to us, calls to us, in the eyes of the needy, in the eyes of laughing children, in the averted eyes of people who think they want to be anonymous and safe from either pain or love.

In the same way, we have all kinds of ways of talking to God that are lying all over the place, ready-to-hand, if we have the sensitivity to notice them and the imagination to turn them into prayers. Anyone who has seen the serigraph posters of Corita Kent knows that even Wonder Bread jingles can be turned into visual prayers. It takes a little tinkering but, with the right understanding, some of the billboard slogans along the highway can turn into secret messages between me and God, like "You only go around once in life, so grab for all the gusto you can get." That could be saying, as Jesus did, "I have come to set fire on the earth," or "I have come that they may have life, and have it more abundantly."

Songs

Not many people realize that the Anthony Newley-Leslie Bricusse song, "Who Can I Turn To?" was not originally intended as a song sung by a man to a woman or a woman to a man. In fact it was a prayer addressed to God. There are other obvious songs that one can turn into prayers without any difficulty at all: "I Don't Know How to Love Him" from *Jesus Christ Superstar*, many of the songs of Simon and Garfunkel and the Beatles, especially something like George Harrison's "My Sweet Lord."

But there are other songs that merely have to capitalize the "You" and they become prayers. For old-timers like me, George Gershwin and Lorenz Hart and Cole Porter are treasure-houses: "I'll be seeing you, in all the old familiar places . . ." and "You are the promised touch of springtime, that makes the lonely winter seem long," and "You're the top!" They were all written originally as a song for two lovers, but what else is prayer?

Pause for a moment, and let your mind ramble over your favorite secular songs. Five'll getcha ten you can think of one that can be turned into a prayer before a couple of minutes are up.

The Newspaper

Even the daily paper can be used as a way God speaks to us, and it can provide subject matters for all kinds of conversation with him. Just as Yahweh spoke to Israel through the plagues of Egypt and the invasions of the Romans, our Father still speaks to us through the events of this week's history. Every picture of urban blight or ecological corruption says the same thing that God said to Adam when he gave him dominion over the earth. Every picture from Southeast Asia or the Middle East is another call to "beat your swords into plowshares" or you will have more of this. Every two-page supermarket ad says, "I was hungry . . . I was naked . . . did you even notice?"

A very strong caution here, however. Someone who becomes aware of the worldwide suffering of mankind is in danger of what has been called "the liberal guilt complex." I think that schools also, with the very best of intentions, very unwisely generate this unfocused, low-grade guilt in us which can stir up a nameless frustration within us and thereby spoil whatever effectiveness we might have had. "What are you doing about those poor starving babies in the Sahara? What are you doing for the orphans of Southeast Asia? What are you doing about wars and famine and ecology and crime in the streets and mental illness and the birthrate and obscenity and . . ." You get to the point where you want to scream: "STOP! I have only two hands and one heart! I have only a twenty-four hour day and perhaps a seventy-year life! I can be in only one place at a time! I *can't* take care of all those things. My God, the President of the United States can't make a dent in even a few of them!" And so we give up.

Such people should be assured that they can't expect themselves to feel responsible for everything, but they should also be reminded that they are responsible for what they *can* do, for the time they *can* carve out from their legitimate recreations to help the needy. If we narrow our attentions to one or two needy areas, we'll be doing just fine.

The purpose of letting the newspaper reveal God to us is that it opens our eyes, scales down our own small troubles closer to the proportions they have in God's eyes, sensitizes us to those in need who *are* within our reach.

Just once, try reading the daily newspaper the way you would expect Jesus Christ would read the newspaper. Try to feel the way he would feel, and then pray the way he would pray. He was a realist, remember. He did not try to take over the centers of power and communications in Rome. He lived in a little backwater of a place and physically touched relatively few people. And yet what he began has changed the world, and it has lasted for twenty centuries. That itself is worth praying over.

"Prayers that Were Never Meant to Be"

The idea for such prayers came to me through Betsy Caprio in her fine booklet, *Experiments in Prayer*. It consists, quite simply, in finding prayers in the least likely places—novels, poems, plays, advertisements—like the visual prayers of Corita Kent. The one I like best is one that apparently flashed out at her from the dull pages of a French grammar book and which she turned into an unexpected little speech to God: "I love you. I have loved you. I will love you." Like finding prayers in popular songs, it is not at all difficult—if you are attuned to look—to find prayers in whatever you read.

The poems of e. e. cummings are a forest of prayers—if a bit thorny to grasp at times. But the very thorniness makes the poem a kind of koan, which can be mulled and distilled and made to seep into the spirit.

> no time ago
> or else a life
> walking in the dark
> i met christ
>
> jesus)my heart
> flopped over
> and lay still
> while he passed(as
>
> close as i'm to you
> yes closer
> made of nothing
> except loneliness
>   e.e. cummings

> i thank You God for most this amazing
> day:for the leaping greenly spirits of trees
> and a blue true dream of sky;and for every thing
> which is natural which is infinite which is yes
>
>
> (i who have died am alive again today,
> and this is the sun's birthday;this is the
> birth-
> day of life and of love and wings:and of the
> gay
> great happening illimitably earth)
>
> how should tasting touching hearing seeing

breathing any—lifted from the no
of all nothing—human merely being
doubt unimaginable You?

(now the ears of my ears awake and
now the eyes of my eyes are opened)

e.e. cummings

The last two lines of that poem are about as good a description of meditative prayer as I have ever read. It is a realization which a very good actor once shared with me about plays: "God is the only one who creates anything; we—even artists—do not create; we merely discover."

Everyone should find his own, but here are some I have found:

I was trying to make my mouth *say* I would do the right thing and the clean thing, and go and write to that nigger's owner and tell where he was; but deep down in me I knowed it was a lie, and He knowed it. You can't pray a lie—I found that out.

—Mark Twain

Everyone in the world is Christ and they are all crucified.

—Sherwood Anderson

i have noticed that when chickens quit quarreling over their food they often find that there is enough for all of them i wonder if it might not be the same with the human race

—Don Marquis

When custom presses on the souls apart,
Who seek a God not worshipped by the
herd,
Forth, to the wilderness the chosen start
Content with ruin, having but the Word.
—John Masefield

There is no indispensable man.
—F. D. Roosevelt

What is man, when you come to think
upon him, but a minutely set, ingenious
machine for turning, with infinite art-
fulness, the red wine of Shiraz into urine?
—Isak Dinesen

For man, the vast marvel is to be
alive. . . . We ought to dance with rapture
that we should be alive and in the flesh, and
part of the living incarnate cosmos. I am
part of the sun as my eye is part of me.
That I am part of the earth my feet know
perfectly, and my blood is part of the sea.
My soul knows that I am part of the
human race, my soul is an organic part of
the great human race, as my spirit is part
of my nation. In my very self, I am part of
my family.
—D. H. Lawrence

Among animals, one has a sense of
humor.
—Marianne Moore

Our lives are merely strange dark in-
terludes in the electrical display of God the
Father!
—Eugene O'Neill

It is better to know some of the questions than all of the answers.

—James Thurber

God is verb,
Not a noun.

—Buckmister Fuller

I have had a good many more uplifting thoughts, creative and expansive visions—while soaking in comfortable baths or drying myself after bracing showers—in well-equipped American bathrooms than I have ever had in any cathedral.

—Edmund Wilson

I believe that man will not merely endure: he will prevail.

—William Faulkner

The Future is something which everyone reaches at the rate of sixty minutes an hour, whatever he does, whoever he is.

—C. S. Lewis

If you forgive people enough you belong to them, and they to you, whether either person likes it or not—squatter's rights of the heart.

—James Hilton

It is often easier to fight for principles than to live up to them.

—Adlai Stevenson

Work

Even Our Lady didn't spend the entire day with all her thoughts on Jesus; there were floors to scrub.

St. Teresa of Avila, a real heavyweight in praying, had to haul herself out of her cell and sit for hours listening with her whole attention to the problems of her nuns. Thomas Merton, the great Trappist monk, had to limit his time of actual meditation because he was not only expected to turn out books but also to take a hand at washing the dishes and hoeing the fields in his monastery. Even people whose prayer-lives are light years ahead of our own had to take their direct awareness away from God and turn it back to the world God gave us to be enlivened.

But our work, too, can be sharing aliveness with God. The daily round of school work or housework or office work or manual work is a contact with surfaces under which lurks the life-giving presence of God, waiting to be noticed, to be brought closer to the surface in everything we do. But how?

Well, the first step is the realization that God *is* truly in all things, even in unpleasant things like memorizing French irregular verbs or cleaning up after the dog or typing lists or sweeping streets. Then, in the times we take for meditative prayer, the task is really to find him there—and in the more unpleasant jobs, the more boring jobs, that task of unearthing the presence of God can sometimes begin to look like a real game of hide-and-seek—when the other Player has given up and gone home.

At times like that, I think, one must begin by trying to find some inner value in the job itself. *Why* am I being asked to memorize these French words, when I'll very likely never go to France? If the only reason you can come up with is, "Oh, well, because 'they' told me I have to," or "*Every*body has to do it," then you're not there yet. *Why* do "they" tell you to and *why* does everybody have to?

The same is true of moving the same dust from the same furniture day after day after day. The same is true of hammering nails or turning a lathe or operating a computer. If the only reason is that someone will gripe if you don't do it or, "What the hell, it's a way to get a paycheck," you're not there yet. Nor is the reason, "Because God asked me to." If the only reason for doing a job comes from outside the job, then there will be little more aliveness or joy or even simple satisfaction in your work than a horse finds pulling a cart or a teletype machine takes from spitting out coded tape.

Why do you do the jobs you do? Only each individual knows what those jobs are, and only each individual can unearth the deepest reasons why he or she does them. Well?

Once you find the true inner purpose of the jobs you "have" to do, a purpose that satisfies not just the surface of your mind but the depths of your heart, you will almost automatically find a newer, richer *quality* in your work. The man who sees not just a paycheck but people's lives improved by his work will not go at it like a zombie. A woman who gets inside her husband's shoes as he returns from work at night, who understands, will not be content with TV dinners. Kahlil Gibran said, "Work is love made visible." And if it's not, the job either shouldn't be done or should be reassessed. If your job is to clean public rest rooms, clean those rooms as if the people you love best were going to use them.

After all, if I understand Jesus Christ rightly, no matter who uses them they will be your brothers and sisters.

Once you begin to go at the dishes or the attic or the weekend composition the way you suspect Jesus Christ would have done them, you will begin to see that Presence emerging even from the most unpromising places, even from the most boring tasks, because in order to draw that Aliveness to the surface some of your own aliveness must be put into it from this side.

Our Father is helplessly in love with aliveness. He cannot resist coming forward to meet it, especially when it is aliveness expended in apparently unpromising places or with unpromising people. Consider what he was able to do with the grumbling slaves of Egypt. Consider what he was able to do with a stable at Bethlehem. Consider what he was able to do with a backwoods rabbi from Nazareth. Consider what he was able to do with a Criminal's execution. He won't be outdone in sharing aliveness.

This transformation of work into prayer—into sharing aliveness with God—has to come first from seeing a reason within the work itself, not by pouring the Morning Offering over it like so much chocolate syrup and then grumbling your way through it like a slave. But once you have seen the inner value that any work has (or else it isn't worth doing), no matter how tedious or endless, then it does help to snatch moments to realize that you are not alone in doing it, that there is another Person at your side, attentive and caring.

It's good to begin the first job of the morning

with a moment of re-collection of self and of the Aliveness within you. Then again after your coffee break, and again after lunch. But this shouldn't become the half-hearted, no-minded formality that most of us associate with the flash of Grace Before Meals or the droning mind-in-neutral prayers before class in school. Those are so often times when the words are said by someone else, while I spend the time wondering whether there are enough pieces of chicken or whether the teacher will call on me today. I remember at the beginning of this year, while I was brushing my teeth, trying to say the Morning Offering and realizing that I couldn't get past "in union with the sacrifice of the Mass throughout the world." I knew there was something about the Pope's intentions at the end but, for the life of me, I couldn't remember the words of a prayer I'd "said" all my life and heard read over the P.A. every single school day for the last nine years! And I began to understand that I hadn't *said* the prayer at all for over a decade; I had merely been present in a room while it "happened."

The prayer at the beginning of a segment of work should not merely be a "prayer," as a child would understand that word, some memorized thing to scoot through the back rooms of one's mind while you're taking the cover off the typewriter or mixing the orange juice. It should be an attempt of the mind and heart, the self, to focus into conscious awareness the Presence Who will do the day's work with you. It's only a moment, but if it's important and prayer has some special place of its own later in your day, you'll remember to do it each time you enter a new phase of the day.

Then once the "connection" has been made, you will forget God no doubt, just as a boy can stare with utter intensity at the gorgeous girl across the aisle while the teacher is handing out the final exam, but once the exam's begun, she could be Godzilla for all he knows; he has more important—or at least more immediately pressing—things on his mind right now.

These are only a few ways in which one can transform the objects and events and persons of every day into a sharing of aliveness with God. Like every artist, he is lurking inside everything he has made, waiting to be noticed and to be "connected with." Everything speaks of him and to him, if "the ears of my ears awake . . . the eyes of my eyes are opened."

PRAYING TOGETHER

Most of us are shy. In fact, I'd be willing to bet that, under even the most brassy and cocksure exteriors, we are *all* basically shy. It takes at least a bit of gumption to say to somebody we don't know very well, "Hey! Howdja like to go to a movie?" We all can imagine, then, the inner fears that would haunt us if we thought of going up to even a good friend and saying, "Hi! Howdja like to pray?"

Praying together is something we'd all more or less rather leave to the packed anonymity of Sunday Mass. Which is precisely why so many people find Sunday Mass boring: it is packed and anonymous, uptight and not personally involving. If you could ever find a congregation, however small, that would be willing to let down defenses and really release its inner power in unashamed sharing of prayer, the church finally would be in danger of really setting the earth on fire as it was told to. No one would leave that congregation and say, "The Church really ought to . . ." They would say instead, "*We* ought to . . ." since they would realize not just in their minds but in the very depths of themselves that we *are* the Church.

Sunday Masses should be a sharing of prayer. Let's face it: in 99 percent of the cases, it isn't. It may well be a few hundred people who gather together and pray silently within themselves, one-on-one with God and also obediently, if half-heartedly, interrupt their "real praying" to moo back answers to the priest. But it's really the priest's show, right? Recently he's been given a few co-stars to read a bit and tell people when to stand and sit (which they already know), but in general all the action is really "up there," isn't it? Sadly, that's not the way the first Mass was, nor is it how all its repetitions were intended to be.

It would be so exciting if each member of the congregation would get involved! But that's not very likely. I remember in college when we were trying to get a friend of ours to cut a class one Friday and hitch with us to a basketball game in Boston. He said, "Weeeeeellll. If you can get six or eight other guys to do it, I'll think about it." From that moment onward, his name was "Guts." The same thing is true of making Mass come alive. If everyone else throws off his uptightness—the way people do at a rock concert—I'm perfectly willing to let down my defenses, too; then I'll have the guts. But instead we cringe when Dad sings so loud, and Mom utters the prayers so audibly. Easier to stand at the back. After all, nobody else is dropping his guard; why should I? And personally, I would lay a great deal of blame for this on the priest who is leading the congregation. If he's as formal as a visiting diplomat, it's little wonder that men and women who have shared the same bed for twenty years will turn to one another at the greeting of peace and *shake hands*!

Because of this reluctance we all seem to share, it may seem quite difficult to entertain the possibility of sharing prayer in a small group. However, it really is nowhere near as intimidating as it sounds. Many people who "teach" methods of prayer often begin with this kind of prayer, reading a passage of Scripture, pausing for personal reflections and then —if anyone wishes—he or she may express a prayer out loud. It's my opinion, though, that it might be better to allow the participants to get a bit more used to personal meditative prayer itself before adding the additional hesitation of doing it with others. Once one has mastered a bit the processes of relaxing, focusing the consciousness, and remaining for awhile in silence without uneasiness, then I believe shared prayer will be not only unintimidating but a real new breakthrough.

As with Mass, there are several practical advantages of praying together. For one thing, it keeps you at it even at times when you are just about ready to throw it away as a bad job—which is precisely the time that most people who doggedly persist at it break through to a new and higher plateau in their prayer. As with having an advisor about your own prayer, praying in a small group with others is also reassurance that you are not alone in believing, in praying, and in trying to continue and grow in prayer.

But over and above the merely practical advantages, shared prayer can be a very enriching experience. Every time I have done it, I've come away enlivened by the honesty and self-forgetfulness of the people with whom I have prayed. It takes any of us a bit of self-exposure to speak aloud the things that we have formerly shared only with God. But overcoming that fear can itself give you a jubilant feeling. And, of course, if one is frightened, then he or she has not really heard the message of the Gospels, which says we should not be afraid. Jesus' first word on entering a room was, "Peace!" He said that those who trusted in him and in his Spirit would be able to handle serpents and cast out devils. Next to that, praying aloud together looks relatively easier.

On the one hand, such prayer sessions should not be the occasion for dredging up one's deepest problems; they take too much explanation, and these meetings are for prayer, not for a psychiatric examination. On the other hand, they should not be merely prayers off the top of the head for the poor and unwanted—like many of the offertory petitions at Mass. This is not "general prayer" like that; it is personal prayer, and what one says should echo up from the real depths of himself. Just as in personal private prayer one wants to contact his genuine and undisguised self, so too in personal shared prayer. One can be truly personal and genuine in this somewhat public prayer without either baring his inmost secrets or hiding behind generalities. Moreover, the Scripture passage or reading gives a kind of center around which the prayers will often satellize.

How To

The first thing to find when a small group of people want to try praying together is a suitable room. If at all possible, it should not be too big. (Nor should the group.) It is good, too, if the room is as far as possible from the loudest distractions and is able to be darkened if the group wants that. However, if the participants have had some experience of private meditation, they should be a bit more adept than most at shutting out distracting noises—passing airplanes, voices down the hall. After awhile, such distractions can be no more audible than a voice telling you to take out the garbage when you are engrossed in music or a television program. Still, it is best to avoid as much noise as possible. Make sure there's a sign on the door telling potential intruders to get lost. And if there's a phone in the room, take it off the hook.

If the room has a rug, so much the better. If individuals want them and they are storable in the place, have pillows and chairs so that people may assume whatever position they find most conducive to peace and concentration. If there are no pillows, people can bundle up their jackets and use them. Take off your shoes and your watches. If you have to limit the time, put an alarm clock in a drawer where you can't hear the ticking.

Sometimes it helps to sit in a circle with a lighted candle in the center. The candle helps concentration, and it keeps the more wary from wondering if "they're all looking at me." But if someone finds it better to sit facing the wall, let him.

As in all times of meditative prayer, take a few moments to do the relaxing exercises—especially here when potential distractions are multiplied and uptightness may make some focus on their own surface uneasiness rather than on their deepest selves. Be sure that each one concentrates his awareness not only on his own deepest self and on the Aliveness that dwells there, but also on the other selves who are sitting in the room and on the intensification of the Presence because of this sharing. "Where two or more are gathered together in my name, there am I in the midst of them."

Then let someone either read a very short passage from the Scriptures or a poem, or play a very short song or some evocative music. Any of the methods suggested in these pages can be used, and God knows there are thousands more. When this initial exercise is finished, let everyone just sit and reflect, ponder and pray. It's wise not to "burst into words" too soon. Let things sift and mull and enliven before they are shared. Then, if the Spirit moves anyone, let him or her express a short prayer out loud—not to the group but to the Presence who hovers in their midst. And those sitting around can share it. If God can speak to us through nature and through words on a page, surely he can speak to us through the mouths of our brothers and sisters.

There are several worries not to be worried. Don't worry that someone will be designated to speak first, or that if the person next to me prays aloud, I'm "on deck" and had better get some whipperdoo of a prayer ready. It is only the Spirit who designates, within each one, when to speak; speak only when—and if—you are moved to. Don't try to confound those nearby with the profundity of your wisdom or with the golden phrases that tumble from your mouth. Keep it simple—simple as the prayer of a child to his Father in the presence of his brothers and sisters. Let the words be ordinary, everyday, unpretentious, from the heart.

Above all, don't use the time of shared prayer to give a long, moralizing lecture or "subtle sermon" on "what we all ought to do." Not only are these ordinarily tedious and at times unconsciously condescending, but they tend to focus the attention of the group on the speaker instead of on the Listener. This is the only thing I believe someone should speak to a member of the group about—outside the session and privately, of course. Whoever has the love and courage to mention it should say, in as kindly a way as he or she can, that this person's longish prayers make the others a bit fidgety. If the person is as sincere as his prayers claim, he will understand and keep them short. If not, as St. Benedict says, "Let two stout monks attempt to reason with him."

Let no one feel he *has* to say something, or that he has to be sure to get a vocalized prayer in on every occasion. If someone says nothing, don't worry about him, and don't feel that the silence has to go on and on until the last one finally gets something out. He may be too shy or too deeply touched or completely involved with the Presence; the Spirit will move each one in a unique way. Besides, saying to yourself, "Well, So-and-So has prayed, and So-and-So, and So-and-So. That leaves . . ." the prayer becomes not prayer but competition and checklisting, like an army roll call. Which is precisely what all of you came to this place to forget for awhile.

Also, don't fear long pauses. For some reason, we fear empty air as if it were the same thing as "dead air" to a radio station engineer. It's not dead at all but very much alive. On the other hand, no one should be afraid that, "I've had my turn, so I'd better shut up and not intrude again, even though what I feel is busting to be said." Unlike lightning, the Spirit can strike as often as he chooses in the same place.

The last thing one should fear is "what they think of me or of what I'm saying or of the way I'm saying it." As the Gospel says, the Spirit will tell you what to say and how to say it.

Jesus said it all in four words: "Do not be afraid."

And let the very last word be his, too: "Peace."